JUSTICE FOR CANADA'S

ABORIGINAL PEOPLES

Renée Dupuis
Translated by Robert Chodos and Susan Joanis

James Lorimer & Company Ltd., Publishers
Toronto 2002

James Lorimer & Company Ltd. acknowledges the support of the Ontario Arts Council. We acknowledge the support of the Government of Canada, through the Book Publishing Industry Development Programs (BPIDP), for our publishing activities. We acknowledge the support of the Canada Council for the Arts for our publishing program.

National Library of Canada Cataloguing in Publication

Dupuis, Renée
    Justice for Canada's Aboriginal peoples / Renée Dupuis ; translators, Robert Chodos and Susan Joanis.

Includes bibliographical references.
ISBN 1-55028-775-3

    1. Indians of North America—Canada—Government relations—1951-.
2. Indians, Treatment of—Canada. 3. Indians of North America—Canada—
Social conditions. 4. Indians—Rehabilitation—Canada. I. Chodos, Robert,
1947-
II. Joanis, Susan III. Title.

| E92.D87213 2002 | 323.1'197071 | C2002-904239-9 |

James Lorimer & Company Ltd., Publishers
35 Britain St.
Toronto, Ontario
M5A 1R7
www.lorimer.ca

Printed and bound in Canada

TABLE OF CONTENTS

INTRODUCTION

When other Canadians hear what Aboriginal people have to say about
Canadian society, they increasingly take it as a rejection. Aboriginals are
clearly very critical of the system that has been imposed on them, and
are unwilling to be led by others or confined to the margins of society.
To the great surprise of Canadians in general, Aboriginal people see
Canadian society very differently than they do. These two divergent
views are based on living conditions that are radically different and —
it must be said — put Aboriginal people at a disadvantage in many
ways. Canadian citizens, comforted by Canada's favourable image on
the international scene, see their living conditions as being almost
without parallel elsewhere in the world, while Aboriginals, encouraged
by growing international concern for indigenous people, see their living conditions as a disgrace.

If we are short of solutions to Aboriginal problems right now, the
reason is largely rooted in the clash of these two opposing perceptions.
Previously the Aboriginal position was expressed in a vacuum and was
not widely heard. The two perceptions of Canadian society developed
in parallel, isolated from each other, to the point where Canadians in
general were barely aware of the widening gap between their living conditions and those of Aboriginal people. As a result, Aboriginals' criticism of the present situation and especially the radicalization of their
rhetoric were greeted with incredulity, incomprehension and frustration. The terse opinions and judgements coming from both sides are
expressions of this state of affairs. We should not be surprised to find
ourselves, at the beginning of the twenty-first century, confronted with
a wall of mutual misunderstanding when it comes to Aboriginal questions.

Obviously, these attitudes are not helping to improve relations at all
— on the contrary, they are encouraging both sides to harden their

positions. This is a potentially explosive situation if nothing is done to defuse it. Conflicts such as the ones that developed at Kanesatake-Oka, Quebec, in 1990, at Gustafsen Lake, British Columbia, and Ipperwash, Ontario, in 1995, and at Burnt Church, New Brunswick, in 1999 and 2000, are tragic examples of the recent deterioration of relations between Aboriginal people and the rest of society. This situation inevitably challenges us, whether we are Aboriginal or not. It is an illusion to think that the passage of time alone will resolve the misunderstanding, if efforts are not made to educate the Canadian population as a whole and raise people's consciousness about Aboriginal reality.

More and more people ask me why we are in this quandary, and many express the hope that it will simply go away on its own. However, an awareness is emerging that we will not be able to ignore Aboriginal reality indefinitely. The aim of this book is to provide some reference points that will allow the reader to understand the current situation better and to define the elements of a program that will end the isolation of Aboriginal people and advance the discussions and negotiations that need to take place. The perspective here is my own. It is not that of Aboriginal people, with whom I have worked for twenty-five years, although it is enriched by the knowledge that my work with them has allowed me to acquire. The analysis is informed by positions that Aboriginal people have taken but that have often had limited impact even when they have been expressed publicly.

Aboriginals have been subordinated and marginalized by successive Canadian governments, and they still are. The growing media attention paid to Aboriginal problems forces us to confront this situation and to face the frustration of Aboriginal people. Because the media have very effective means at their disposal to reach Canadian households, this attention has at least one positive effect: It has become very difficult to feign ignorance of these problems, even if their causes and origins are not being adequately explained.

Aboriginal people have been given a special status in Canadian society, which in practice is a second-class status. In this book, I look at some of the many forms this second-class status has taken. Aboriginals have always challenged this state of affairs, and they are now doing so with increasing vehemence. Their numerous demands and grievances are consequential for the future of Canadian society. They are inviting us to bring about radical political change while at the same time demanding compensation for the damages that their subordination has caused them. By looking at their deplorable socioeconomic conditions, we can grasp the extent of the social disarray that the system imposed on them has brought about. Recent indicators are clear expressions of this situation.

Canadian society needs to take responsibility for its treatment of Aboriginal people and take account of their hopes and goals. To do this, we need a complete change in perspective in our relations with them. There are paths we can take that will allow us to achieve this essential reorientation. We will also see that as a result of globalization, new possibilities for reflection and action on the international level have opened up, both for governments and for Aboriginal people. The questions we are examining are now global ones, and this new scope has inevitable repercussions for the way we address these questions. While in 1990 the Kanesatake-Oka crisis was seen as a matter internal to Quebec, such a perspective is no longer possible. Nor can we address Aboriginal questions on a purely Canadian level. For one thing, Aboriginal people in Canada will take initiatives to enhance the international impact of these questions. In addition, gains made in one country become objectives for indigenous people elsewhere to attain.

It also seems clear to me that Aboriginal people have a responsibility to develop their objectives and to work with society as a whole to achieve them, for the cooperation of all Canadians will be needed to reach those objectives. We need a parallel movement, with each party performing the tasks that are incumbent on it. But these parallel tasks need to converge towards a common enterprise if we wish to narrow the gulf between the two parties. In this context, polarization of the discussion will not be easy to resist.

Public opinion has begun to evolve. More and more news reports about Aboriginal problems are appearing in the media, and increasing numbers of serious questions are being asked about the nature of these problems. People are showing signs of a more realistic attitude towards their complexity, perhaps based on a recognition that caricatures don't resolve anything and can contribute to making the situation worse. A new awareness is emerging that we need to understand what could have caused society to reach a crisis point. This is a first, and determining, step towards the development of relations that will be fundamentally different from the ones that have prevailed until now.

FOREWORD TO THE ENGLISH EDITION

According to a study published in the summer of 2002, average life expectancy for Canadians is seventy-eight years. Breaking down this overall figure reveals significant differences, from a peak in Richmond, B.C., where residents can expect to live to eighty-one, to a low among the Inuit of Nunavik, in northern Quebec, whose lives will likely not go beyond age sixty-five. This is just one of many indicators that demonstrate the huge gap in life chances among Canadians, depending on whether one belongs to an Aboriginal group or not. How can we account for this gap?

Many other questions can be asked as well. Aside from the fact that both have been high-profile media events, what does the "lobster crisis" that has been going on in Burnt Church, New Brunswick, since 1999 have in common with the 2002 treaty referendum held in British Columbia on the heels of that province's agreement with the Nisga'a, reached in 1998? What role did the Supreme Court of Canada play in these two series of events? More precisely, what was the effect of two Supreme Court rulings — one in 1973, concerning the Aboriginal rights of the Nisga'a in British Columbia, and another in 1999, regarding rights of the Mi'kmaq First Nations in New Brunswick flowing from a historic treaty between these First Nations and the British crown? Why is it that the situation of Aboriginal people in Canada requires an analysis that, while taking provincial and regional particularities into account, transcends these particularities?

Using its constitutional authority, the federal government tabled two bills directly affecting First Nations in June 2002. The first, Bill C-60, is aimed at establishing the Canadian Centre for the Independent Resolution of First Nations Specific Claims. This centre, which will include a commission and a tribunal, constitutes a major change in Canadian policy. The government is now prepared to give a tribunal the final say in determining the validity of claims based on a failure to honour treaties signed with First Nations communities or poor administration of First Nations land and funds. It will also be able to award compensation of up to $7 million for those claims. The centre will replace the Indian Claims Commission, set up in 1991 in the aftermath of the "Oka crisis." Ottawa is thus responding to numerous criticisms that have been levelled against it since it adopted its Specific Claims Policy in 1973. Under this policy, it acts as both judge and interested party by deciding on validity, negotiations and compensation for a given claim.

The other bill, C-61, aims to "provide" the tools of governance to First Nations until such time as the inherent right to self-government, recognized in principle by this government, is negotiated and put into practice. This is the latest attempt to change the Indian Act, which lays out the guardianship system under which First Nations communities are governed. The government is not proposing meaningful, in-depth reforms to the Indian Act, but rather replacing certain parts and introducing new obligations of transparency and accountability for First Nations leaders on reserves. These new obligations affect methods of choosing leaders, internal governance and financial management. Although the bill has wider implications, it can be seen as the government imposing new constraints on Indian bands in return for establishing an independent settlement mechanism for specific claims.

Bill C-61 also makes provision for another significant measure. If it is adopted into law, First Nations people will be able to exercise their right to protection from discrimination under the Canadian Human Rights Act, something they have not been able to do since the act was passed in 1978. Thus, federal government and band council immunity will be lifted, as recommended by an advisory committee on changes to the act (of which I was a member) in its June 2000 report to the minister of justice.

In June 2002, the federal Indian Affairs Minister Robert Nault also announced the establishment of a working group to consult on education issues for First Nations, and the eventual tabling of additional legislation aimed at establishing separate financial institutions for First Nations.

The First Nations have persistently opposed changes recommended by Ottawa ever since Jean Chrétien, as minister of Indian affairs, tried to repeal the Indian Act in 1969. This opposition continued vociferously throughout the past year, even as the current minister of Indian affairs held consultations on the new bill. As Bill C-61 reached the House of Commons in June 2002, some First Nations spokespeople condemned it for perpetuating Canada's "colonialism" towards them. They were simply reiterating the charge made by Matthew Coon-Come, National Chief of the Assembly of First Nations of Canada, at the international conference on racism in Durban, South Africa, in 2001. Coon-Come stated that Canada had imposed a "colonialist" regime on First Nations people. Prime Minister Chrétien's swift reaction reflected the shock many Canadians felt at these words. How is it that Aboriginals and other Canadians have such vastly different perspectives on our society?

The terrible conditions in which Aboriginals in Canada live call out to all Canadians. Achieving the changes necessary for addressing these conditions will require attention from the federal government, provincial governments and First Nations communities alike. Imposing new rules for public administration cannot serve as a panacea. Members of Aboriginal communities still need to become active players in defining and establishing such rules. The legitimacy of new regulations will be as important as their legality. Will these new initiatives create the conditions needed to bring about the radical changes that will allow Aboriginal people to take full responsibility for their present and their future? What are those conditions? The discussion that follows is an exploration of these questions.

Renée Dupuis
July 2002

CHAPTER 1

Disadvantaged and Apart

M easures taken by successive governments have contributed to the marginalization of Aboriginal people. In the 1960s, federal representatives unequivocally acknowledged this situation. Indian Affairs Minister Jean Chrétien, announcing the new Indian policy that Ottawa sought to implement in 1969, expressed the view that the special relations Canadian society had established with Indians since the time of earliest European settlement had "made of the Indians a community disadvantaged and apart."[1] Even at that time, Chrétien — who would later become prime minister of Canada — asked whether this major component of the Canadian population would participate fully in the general welfare or whether social and economic disparities, substantial in the 1960s, would become even more pronounced. At the same time, he recognized that if inequality did increase, it would "lead to their increasing frustration and isolation, a threat to the general well-being of society."[2] It is difficult not to agree with Chrétien's statement of the time that government policies "have kept the Indian people apart from and behind other Canadians."[3] It is not a coincidence that three decades later, as prime minister, he announced that the problems of Aboriginal people would be one of his government's major concerns in the third term that he won in his election victory in the fall of 2000.

The social and political marginalization of Aboriginal people

Today, we have a greater appreciation of the ways in which their special relationship with Canadian society has contributed to the marginalization of Aboriginal people, especially Indians. The lands that they occupied were taken to be used for settlement and development. They had no access to the profits from the resources that these lands contained, so that their economic independence was significantly compromised. Whatever the original motivation for such a policy, Canada's historical and present-day development appears to be founded on a conception of Aboriginal people as obstacles to be cleared from the road toward economic growth and exploitation of the land's resources.

The decision to establish reserves was made with the aim of civilizing Aboriginal people as a prelude to integrating them into society, but it had the effect of isolating them. This isolation strengthened their cultural identity, distinct from that of Europeans and Canadians. Forcing Aboriginals to become sedentary peoples on reserves allowed them to maintain and develop their particular characteristics. Conditions were created that favoured emphasizing the differences between them and other Canadians. The vaunted superiority of European cultures led to a policy of seeking to assimilate Aboriginal people, but the means chosen to implement this policy allowed Aboriginal culture to survive and even continue to develop. The paradox is that these means had the effect of creating a heightened perception among Aboriginals of their own identity.

The replacement of traditional authorities in Aboriginal communities accelerated the destabilization of those communities. Subordinated to the authority of governments, they were stripped of responsibility for their present and future and made dependent on government measures and subsidies. Aboriginal populations were displaced and turned into sedentary communities. The ostensible goal was to improve their living conditions, but in practice they were kept in material conditions that other citizens would not have accepted.

Aboriginal people were not allowed to vote until 1960 at the federal level and even later in some provinces, such as Quebec. Their disenfranchisement not only deprived them of a fundamental right but also perpetuated the perception that Indian status was an inferior status in Canadian democracy. Throughout the pre–1960 period, they had no influence — either directly as members of Parliament or indirectly through legislators they might have voted for — in formulating legislation that was imposed on them. Since they were not full-fledged citizens in society, Indians could not benefit from equal status or equal services. Aboriginal people were left out of the mainstream, and this situation led to a growing misunderstanding between them and the rest of society, which caused considerable frustration on both sides. While many Canadians regarded Aboriginal people as benefiting from a privileged state, they often saw themselves as victims without a future.

People's reluctance to recognize the Aboriginal contribution to the development of Canada, past and present, raises a number of questions. It is remarkable that the reinterpretation of history demanded by Aboriginal people has taken so long to begin. Some Aboriginals are insisting on writing their own history in response to the official version, which reflects the conception that Aboriginal people were destined to become extinct through contact with more "advanced" peoples whose development was based on technological progress. We will return to this subject in chapter 3.

Canadian governments have also so far resisted acknowledging their responsibility for the wrongs caused to Aboriginal people. This resistance reflects a feeling that is not always clearly expressed but is nevertheless widespread among the Canadian population. Governments need to be cautious in situations like this, people say, because acknowledging responsibility leads to compensating the victims for the damages caused. It is true that caution is warranted in this case, as in others where the responsibility of the state is involved. Nevertheless, the Canadian government has acknowledged its responsibility and provided compensation to other groups who have lived through complex experiences, taking legal risks in the process. One need only think of the compensation provided to citizens of Japanese origin who were interned in Canada during the Second World War or to the recipients of tainted blood. When the government does not provide similar compensation to Aboriginal communities, it conveys the impression that Aboriginal problems are of lesser importance and do not require the same degree of corrective action as other problems. The fact that the government of Sweden, for example, acknowledged the wrongs that had been committed against that country's Sami people and formally apologized to them has made Canada's position all the more difficult for Aboriginals to accept.

Social disarray in Aboriginal communities

Countless reports have indicated that living conditions are markedly worse for Aboriginal people than for other Canadians, no matter what province or territory they live in. In some places, Aboriginal people live in conditions so far removed from those of a city in Quebec or a small town in Manitoba that it is hard to believe that they are in the rich country called Canada. This is Canada's Third World. But the fact that Aboriginal people often live below the Canadian standard of comfort and well-being is only part of the story. Socioeconomic statistics indicate the degree to which a number of problems have become endemic among them and reflect a disturbing state of social disarray. To the extent that there has been improvement, it has been primarily in areas related to infrastructure. Better public works and adequate housing will undoubtedly have a major effect on Aboriginal living conditions. The gap to be closed in this area is so large that huge investments will be required. However, even bringing infrastructure in Aboriginal communities up to date so that it meets twenty-first-century standards will not guarantee an improvement in other socioeconomic indicators, as statistics clearly show.

From a number of points of view, other socioeconomic indicators show gaps and lags that are not being quickly resolved, at least among Indians living on reserves and Inuit living in northern villages. For these aspects of Aboriginal life to improve, there will need to be a major effort in these communities, especially in the areas of education, health and social services. This kind of work cannot produce dramatic results in the short term. It means that these communities have to make a major commitment to take responsibility for their problems, and that solutions adapted to their needs have to be worked out and implemented. This represents a large challenge not only for Aboriginal people but also for all Canadians.

The poor conditions in which Aboriginal people live have direct effects both on them and on Canadian society. On one level, the scale of the problems they face has inevitable repercussions for Aboriginal people's perception of their future. It is no accident that Aboriginals of all generations show so many signs of worry and despair about what the future holds in store for them. On another level, this situation has repercussions for Canadian society. It is not in the interest of any society to allow a gulf of this magnitude to be opened up between groups of its citizens, a gulf created by misunderstanding, discriminatory treatment and major inequities in status and living conditions. As frustration is exacerbated on both sides, the risk of conflict grows, and the fact that such conflicts arise from a situation that has been deteriorating for a long time will make them all the more difficult to resolve. So far, these conflicts have not become widespread in Canada, but Canada is no more immune to troubles of this sort than any other society. Of course, the longer this clearly deplorable situation persists, the more Canada's reputation as a country that respects human rights will suffer.

In every statistical report about Aboriginal people, a methodological difficulty arises. Models used to measure the level of well-being in the general population do not provide a sound basis for measuring the elements of well-being in Aboriginal communities. First, Statistics Canada does not include data collected in small communities because the use of such data would compromise the confidentiality of its information. In addition, many Indian bands do not fill out census forms. And then, the Department of Indian and Northern Affairs and Statistics Canada use different criteria in collecting information on Aboriginal populations, so that it is difficult to compare statistics from these two agencies. The Department of Indian and Northern Affairs, which is responsible for Indians and Inuit, compiles statistics on the basis of the legislative criteria that define Indian status and administrative criteria such as whether or not Indians live on a reserve. This distinction is used in a number of the department's statistical compilations, making it difficult to establish an overall picture of the Indian population or to compare it with the Inuit population. Meanwhile, Statistics Canada compiles its data using information collected on the basis of voluntary declarations by people who consider themselves Aboriginal, regardless of whether they meet legislative criteria.

These and other constraints need to be kept in mind in interpreting the results of statistical analyzes. Results obtained on particular Indian reserves cannot easily be generalized to all of them. Models based on income calculations do not take into account the contribution of subsistence hunting and fishing. Nor is there necessarily a consensus on the definition of the concept of poverty, which typically relates to resources available for attaining an adequate standard of living. While "adequate" is defined as the capacity to meet basic needs, there is no clear indication of what constitutes a basic need. Still, underneath these methodological difficulties lies a troubling realization: Every socioeconomic indicator shows that Aboriginal people live in clearly disadvantaged conditions in comparison with the Canadian population as a whole.

In its 1983 report, the special committee of the House of Commons on Indian self-government noted that as a result of government control, established more than a hundred years earlier, Aboriginal people had "moved from self-sustaining First Nations to a state of social disorganization."[4] Its conclusion was based on an accumulation of socioeconomic data that demonstrated the extent of "social disintegration"[5] in Indian communities, as illustrated by the following examples. Average income for Indians was between 50 and 75 per cent of the national average. The suicide rate for Indians was three times the rate for all Canadians, while for young Indians (aged fifteen to twenty-four) it was six times the rate for young Canadians. The infant mortality rate was 60 per cent higher for Indians than for all Canadians. Life expectancy for Indians was ten years below the national average; thus, for Indian women, it was sixty-six years, while for other Canadian women, it was seventy-six years.

Ten years later, official income statistics indicated that almost half of Indian families on reserves were living below the poverty line; this was three times the comparable percentage for all Canadians. The province with the lowest proportion of Aboriginal families living below the poverty line — one family in three — was Quebec. However, this proportion was still almost double the proportion of all Quebec families living below the poverty line. The highest proportion — two of every three Aboriginal families below the poverty line — was found in Nova Scotia. This was four times as high as the proportion for other families in the province. It should be noted that the federal government is responsible for Indians living on reserves, so that these statistics should not be seen as the result of provincial policies that are more effective in some provinces than in others. That is simply not the case. The temptation to applaud the governments of those provinces where the situation is better and blame the governments of those where it is worse needs to be resisted. One fact remains: Aboriginal poverty rates are high in all parts of Canada. In addition, while there is considerable variation from reserve to reserve, poverty was very widespread in Indian reserves in the early 1990s, with one family in two living in poverty in about two-thirds of reserves.

In its special 1995 report on the critical problem of Aboriginal suicide, the Royal Commission on Aboriginal Peoples highlighted the fact that previous reports on this question showed that an abnormally high number of Aboriginal people killed themselves. According to the commission, Aboriginal suicide is a complex question. It clearly has an individual aspect, as suicide is an expression of an individual person's despair. But it also has a collective component, since a high suicide rate in a community has repercussions for the community as a whole.

A highlight of the special report is the startling testimony of Chief Jean-Charles Pietacho on behalf of the Innu-Montagnais of Mingan on Quebec's lower North Shore. Speaking at a public hearing held by the commission in Montreal in 1993, Chief Pietacho painted a sobering picture of "collective despair, or collective lack of hope" and its various manifestations in communities such as his. According to Pietacho,

> Collective despair, or collective lack of hope, will lead
> us to collective suicide. This type of suicide can take

many forms, foreshadowed by many possible signs: identity crisis, loss of pride, every kind of dependence, denial of our customs and traditions, degradation of our environment, weakening of our language, abandonment of our struggle for our Aboriginal rights, our autonomy and our culture, uncaring acceptance of violence, passive acknowledgement of lack of work and unemployment, corruption of our morals, tolerance of drugs and idleness, parental surrendering of responsibilities, lack of respect for elders, envy of those who try to keep their heads up and who might succeed, and so on.[6]

It was probably testimony such as this that led the commission to say that Aboriginal suicide is such a widespread problem because Aboriginal people feel that they are marginalized, excluded from the collective wealth of the country and victimized by institutional racism. The commission recommended an ambitious Framework for Action to deal with the issue.

Responding in 1998 to the royal commission's overall recommendations, the federal government acknowledged that socioeconomic indicators still showed Aboriginal people lagging behind the Canadian population as a whole. The situation is all the more worrisome in that Aboriginal people are the fastest growing group in Canada and about 60 per cent of Indians living on reserves and Inuit are under the age of twenty-five. While the cohort of people sixty-five and over is growing in the population in general, its proportion is diminishing among Aboriginal people. Thus, the age pyramid for Indian and Inuit populations is significantly different from the pyramid for the rest of the Canadian population. These demographic trends have direct consequences for the way demand for goods and services is evolving in the general population. As the proportion of older people in the non-Aboriginal population grows, demand for services will largely be oriented towards this population group. In contrast, among Aboriginal groups, the concentration will need to be on services related to education, training and job development for a rapidly growing young and economically active population.

Eloquent figures

Figures from the 1996 census show 42,000 Inuit living in the northern regions of Canada and 610,784 people with official Indian status living on reserves and elsewhere. While the rate of growth of these two populations is diminishing, it is still significantly higher than the rate for the Canadian population as a whole. The rate of population growth for Indians fell from 5.7 per cent in 1991 to 3.6 per cent in 1996, while the rate for the population as a whole fell from 1.4 to 1.3 per cent in the same period.

The number of registered Indians grew by 20 per cent between 1981 and 1986, from 337,000 to 403,000, while the Canadian population grew by 4 per cent during the same period. Part of this growth occurred because some Indians recovered their status in 1985 after having lost it years earlier, primarily because of a clause in the Indian Act that discriminated against Indian women. Before 1985, an Indian woman who married a non-Indian man lost her status and hence could not transmit it to her children. By contrast, if her brother married a non-Indian woman, he not only kept his status but transmitted it to his wife and children. The reintegration of these Indians who had lost their status had an impact on the figures for a number of years. In 1986, only a year after the act was amended, official statistics already indicated that 18,000 people had been added to the Indian Register.

In a medium-population-growth scenario, the number of Indians living on and off reserves could reach 721,000 in 2011, while in a high-growth scenario — which so far has been the reality — it could reach 764,000 in that year. Another population-growth scenario predicts that the Indian population will reach 822,200 in 2010. The actual 1996 population of 610,784 was higher than the first high-growth scenario, which predicted that the population would reach 580,300 in 1996, and was closer to the second scenario, which predicted a population of 602,700 in 1995. In all probability, population increase will continue to correspond to a high-growth model for a number of years. Table 1 shows an estimate of Indian population increase in a high-growth scenario, based on actual population data since 1985.

Table 1
Estimated Registered Indian Population, On Reserve and Off Reserve,
Canada, 1985–2010 (Projections)

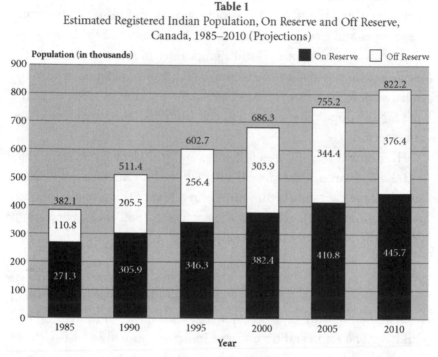

Source: Estimates of Nault et al. (1993). Estimates adjusted to take into account late declaration.

Taken from Canada Department of Indian and Northern Affairs, Research and Analysis Directorate.
Implications of First Nations Demography.

While the Aboriginal fertility rate diminished significantly between 1908 and 1995, there was an average of two children per Indian family in 1996, while the comparable figure for the rest of the population was 1.2. Among both Indians and Inuit, growth in the number of people in their reproductive years largely compensated for the declining fertility rate and contributed to the increasing number of births.

As for family structure, most families had two spouses both among Aboriginals and in the rest of the Canadian population, as table 2 shows. However, the proportion of single-parent families is higher

Table 2
Family Structure, 1991 and 1986
(percentage)

Census Year	Family Structure	Aboriginal	Registered Indian On Reserve	Registered Indian Off Reserve	Inuit	Métis	Non-Aboriginal
1991	Husband-Wife	81.9	77.2	73.4	81.1	74.6	87.3
	Lone Male	2.4	5.6	2.4	4.0	3.7	2.2
	Lone Female	15.7	17.2	24.1	15.9	21.7	10.5
	Total	100.0	100.0	100.0	100.0	100.0	100.0
1986	Husband-Wife	80.7	75.6	70.1	81.0	—	87.5
	Lone Male	2.9	6.6	2.4	5.1	—	2.2
	Lone Female	16.4	17.8	27.5	13.8	—	10.2
	Total	100.0	100.0	100.0	100.0	100.0	100.0

Source: Indian and Northern Affairs, Customized Census Tabulations 1991, 1986.
Note: Figures may not add up to 100 per cent because of rounding.

Taken from Canada. Department of Indian and Northern Affairs. Information Quality and Research Directorate. *Highlights of Aboriginal Conditions 1991, 1986*, p. 67.

among Indians (23 per cent) and Inuit (20 per cent) than in the rest of the population (13 per cent). Among Indians, single-parent families headed by a woman are almost twice as common as in the rest of the population.

Life expectancy for Indian women increased from sixty-six years in the 1980s to seventy-five years in 1996, while life expectancy for all Canadian women increased from seventy-six to eighty-one years in the same period. Thus, although the gap narrowed during the period, there was still a six-year gap in 1996. For Indian men, life expectancy increased from sixty-six years in 1991 to sixty-eight years in 1996, remaining significantly below life expectancy for all Canadian men, which increased from seventy-four to seventy-five years during the same period. With this seven-year gap relative to all Canadian men, Indian men were the group with the shortest life expectancy among all Canadian citizens.

A supplementary indicator of the poor health conditions in Indian communities is the tuberculosis rate, which reflects the material conditions in which Indians live. While Canada has succeeded in keeping tuberculosis in check in the general population, the rate has always been high among Aboriginal people. Although it has declined recently, the tuberculosis rate is still six times as high among Indians living on reserves as it is for the population as a whole, as table 3 shows.

Table 3
Health

	Registered Indians	Registered Indians On Reserve	Total Population of Canada	Registered Indians	Registered Indians On Reserve	Total Population of Canada
	1991			**1996**		
Life Expectancy— Males (Years)	66.9	—	74.6	68.2	—	75.7
Females (Years)	74.0	—	80.9	75.9	—	81.5
Crude Birth Rate (per 1,000)	28.4	—	14.3	25.0	—	12.2
Crude Mortality Rate (per 1,000)	4.3	—	7.0	5.1	—	7.1
Infant Mortality Rate (per 1,000)	11.9	—	6.4	11.6	—	6.1
Total Fertility Rate	2.9	—	1.7	2.7	—	1.7
Age Standardized Tuberculosis Incidence Rate (per 100,000)	—	58.1	7.2	—	35.8	6.5

Taken from Canada. Department of Indian and Northern Affairs. *Comparison of Social Conditions, 1991 and 1996*, p. 5.

Aboriginal people are behind in education as well. Statistics show that Aboriginal people are attending school and graduating at a slightly greater rate than they used to, but they have still not caught up to the national average. In 1996, Canadians were twice as likely as Indians to have completed postsecondary studies: 14 per cent as compared to 7 per cent. As table 4 shows, the proportion of Indians who have had

Table 4
Highest Level of Schooling, Graduates and Non-Graduates, 1991 and 1986
(percentage)

Census Year	Highest Level of Schooling	Aboriginal	Registered Indian On Reserve	Registered Indian Off Reserve	Inuit	Métis	Non-Aboriginal
1991	< Grade 9	18.4	37.2	19.4	47.4	24.8	13.8
	High School	42.8	36.7	44.7	25.6	46.9	38.9
	Non-University	26.5	20.8	24.8	24.7	22.4	26.3
	University	12.3	5.2	11.1	2.3	5.9	21.0
	Total	100.0	100.0	100.0	100.0	100.0	100.0
1986	< Grade 9	28.2	46.4	26.0	55.5	—	18.5
	High School	37.4	33.8	40.7	26.0	—	30.9
	Non-University	23.6	14.6	22.7	14.5	—	28.1
	University	10.8	4.2	10.6	3.9	—	21.4
	Total	100.0	100.0	100.0	100.0	100.0	100.0

Source: Indian and Northern Affairs, Customized Census Tabulations 1991, 1986.
Note: Figures may not add up to 100 per cent because of rounding.

Taken from Canada. Department of Indian and Northern Affairs. Information Quality and Research Directorate. *Highlights of Aboriginal Conditions 1991, 1986*, p. 77.

some postsecondary (including university) education is only about half the proportion in the rest of the population. If we look only at university education, the gap is even wider: Only 5.2 per cent of Indians had some university education, or one-quarter of the Canadian figure of 21 per cent. The 2.3 per cent of Inuit who had some university education was only a tenth of the Canadian percentage. Nor did these students necessarily complete their education. In 1996, only 3 per cent of Indians had received university degrees, compared with 13 per cent of all Canadians.

Income statistics show that the percentage of Indian families living in poverty was still very high in 1995 — 40 per cent. While the number of poor families in Canada increased during the 1990s, the gap between Aboriginal families and all Canadian families remained wide. Aboriginal income levels have been increasing, but the number of poor

Table 5

Income Composition, 1991

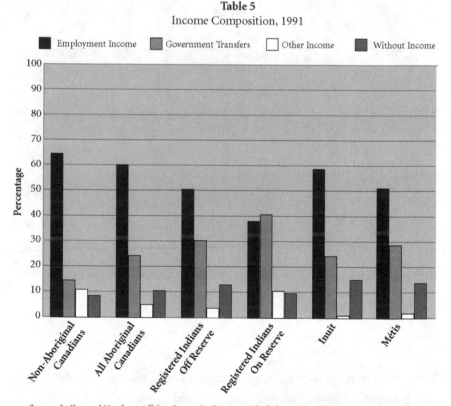

Source: Indian and Northern Affairs, Customized Census Tabulations 1991, 1986.

Taken from Canada. Department of Indian and Northern Affairs. Information Quality and Research Directorate. *Highlights of Aboriginal Conditions 1991, 1986*, p. 99.

families has been increasing as well. Among both Indians and Inuit, the number of families whose main source of income was government transfer payments increased between 1986 and 1991. Transfer payments represented two-fifths of all income for Indians on reserves and one-fourth of all income for Inuit, while the figure for the rest of the population was only one-sixth, as table 5 shows. Employment income represents a very low proportion of income for Indians living on reserves — 39 per cent as compared to 57 per cent for Inuit and 65 per cent for all Canadians.

Income statistics are a reflection of the unemployment rate, which is twice as high among Indians and Inuit as in the rest of the population, in all categories of workers except university graduates. Among Indians living on reserves, it is three times as high as in the rest of the population.

In the area of housing, the government has acknowledged that half of all dwellings on Indian reserves need to be replaced. In 1995, out of the 600 Indian reserves in Canada, 211 drinking water supply systems and sixty-four waste water treatment systems posed serious risks for residents' health. Nor would bringing existing systems up to standard be enough: The pressure of population growth means that substantial new investment is needed. Although the situation has improved significantly since the 1980s, many houses do not have a drinking water supply even now. The proportion of houses with a drinking water supply has increased from 74 to 96 per cent, while waste water treatment systems now serve 92 per cent of houses, up from 67 per cent. Rapid population growth will put considerable pressure on infrastructure costs, as can be seen by the almost 50 per cent rise in infrastructure spending on Indian reserves between 1987 and 1996.

The deplorable living conditions of Aboriginal people in Canada have increasingly come to the attention of international agencies. In 1998 the United Nations Committee on Economic, Social and Cultural Rights found the flagrant disparity between the situation of Aboriginal people and that of most Canadians a source of great concern. Having ratified the International Covenant on Economic, Social and Cultural

Rights, Canada is required to produce periodic reports for the UN on how it protects the rights envisioned in this international agreement.

Analyzing the most recent report submitted by Canada in 1998, the UN committee referred to the first-place status Canada had occupied in the UN's Human Development Index rankings since 1993. This status confirmed that Canadians enjoyed a high standard of living and that Canada had the means to take all necessary measures to ensure the protection of the economic, social and cultural rights guaranteed by the international covenant. However, Canada was only in tenth place in the ranking of the UN's poverty index, which showed that the country was not fully ensuring the protection of these rights. In this regard, the committee saw Aboriginal people as continuing to be disadvantaged on the social and economic levels and said that the situation was not improving. On the basis of Canadian data, the committee highlighted the shortage of adequate housing and the absence of drinking water supply systems (25 per cent of houses needed major repairs and lacked essential facilities in 1998), as well as endemic unemployment and the high suicide rate in Aboriginal communities, especially among young people.

Media coverage of events involving Aboriginal people

Through most of the twentieth century, Aboriginal protests went unnoticed, although government archives bear ample witness to such protests. Aboriginal people were marginalized not only politically and administratively but socially as well, so that until recently their actions had little public impact. There is a clear dividing line between the almost total absence of media coverage of events involving Aboriginal people before the summer of 1990 and media treatment of these questions since that date. More precisely, the dividing line is formed by what came to be called the Oka crisis.

The events that occurred in July 1990 in Kanesatake-Oka surprised almost everyone in Quebec and the rest of Canada. These events immediately followed the rejection of the Meech Lake Accord, which Prime

Minister Brian Mulroney and the provincial premiers had concluded three years earlier with the aim of "reconciling" Quebec with the rest of Canada. Indians were highly critical of the accord, but people paid little attention to their opposition.

Recognition in the 1982 constitution of the existence of Aboriginal peoples in Canada with special collective rights had created great expectations. Constitutional conferences held between 1983 and 1987 were supposed to define Aboriginal peoples' ancestral rights, as well as their newly recognized treaty rights. However, these constitutional discussions did not give Aboriginal people the opportunity to make these concepts specific in the way that they had hoped. With their initial hopes disappointed, Aboriginal people were further frustrated in 1987 when they realized that the federal government was making great efforts to recognize the special status of Quebec in the Canadian constitution while refusing to add any special considerations for them. As the June 1990 deadline for ratification of the Meech Lake Accord approached, Canadians seemed to have forgotten that Aboriginal people saw Meech Lake as a missed opportunity to complete the exercise of defining their rights. This is the context for the opposition of an Indian member of the Manitoba legislature, which became one of the factors in the rejection of Meech Lake.

Extensive media coverage of the Oka conflict, which dragged through many weeks and in the course of which a non-Indian police officer was killed, made people aware of the explosive potential contained in Indian demands. It led people to wonder whether government authorities were adequately prepared to respond to violent situations of this sort and whether sufficient measures were being taken to try to prevent them. In both Quebec and the rest of Canada, shocking images were engraved in the collective imagination through detailed media reports of the violent events involving the Mohawks of Kanesatake and — later in the conflict — of Kahnawake. What emerged from these images as they settled in was an essentially derogatory picture of Indians in Quebec.

For Aboriginal people in Canada, the media coverage made it possible to turn the Mohawks' struggle in Kanesatake into a symbol of Indians' resistance to being dispossessed of their lands. European media, covering media events staged by Mohawks in Europe that summer, also highlighted this symbolic aspect of the conflict. It is significant that the media were not interested in the more fundamental questions underlying the events of the summer of 1990, either during the "crisis" or after it was resolved. For example, the media could have provided information on the Mohawks' traditional demands in the region, the historical links between the Kanesatake and Oka communities and the effects of the crisis on relations between members of the two communities. The role of the federal government in relation to Mohawk territorial demands in the twentieth century and the effects of the rejection of these demands in the years preceding the crisis also deserved media attention. Yet another area that could have been the subject of in-depth media analysis was the role of the Quebec government, its relations with the federal government during the crisis and the reasons for resorting to the Quebec police rather than the Canadian army. In addition, it is remarkable that no links were drawn in 1990 between the events at Oka and events that had occurred a few years earlier in British Columbia, which also involved the expansion of a golf course and led to a very important legal decision in favour of the Indians in 1984.

At the same time, the massive coverage demonstrated the media potential of such events. Contentious incidents involving Aboriginal people could become major media operations and provide prime material for news coverage over an extended period. Media coverage of the crisis also served as a starting point for further media reports, through which Canadians learned that the events in Kanesatake-Oka in the summer of 1990 represented the beginning of a series of violent incidents in various parts of the country: in Gustafsen Lake, British Columbia, in 1995; in Ipperwash, Ontario, also in 1995; and in Burnt Church, New Brunswick, in 1999–2000, to name only a few.

The treatment of Aboriginal questions in the media centres primarily on problems. From a news and public affairs point of view, events in which Aboriginal people are seen to experience problems are more likely to attract attention, and so analyzes of situations related to Aboriginal people are rare outside that context. As many media representatives acknowledge, the media are businesses whose profits are determined by consumer response, which can only be evoked by subjects that are new or shocking. Public broadcasters are on the same wavelength as private ones from this point of view. Consequently, it is not surprising that despite occasional laudable initiatives, information about Aboriginal people that is not sensational is unlikely to be brought to the public's attention. Responsibility for the nature of the coverage is in the hands of media institutions with inordinate power to create and destroy the images that determine how public opinion perceives a particular subject.

As each new crisis involving Aboriginal people is relayed to us, it brings widespread and increasing public irritation to the surface. These crises generally feature Indians rather than Inuit, probably in part because there are more Indians in the more populated areas of the country, and friction is less frequent in the northern regions where the Inuit constitute a majority of the population. It is easy to see that media reports of these crises do not generally provide crucial points of information that would allow public opinion to form an enlightened view of the situation. Because Aboriginal questions are, in most cases, not dealt with outside of news reports, lack of time becomes a pretext for not probing these events. Even when an event lasts several weeks, the media do not take advantage of the opportunity that this gives them to take an in-depth look at the issues.

The "lobster crisis," which centred on fishing by the Mi'kmaq of New Brunswick and began after a Supreme Court of Canada decision in favour of the Mi'kmaq in the fall of 1999, is an eloquent example of this media attitude. The more dramatic aspects of the crisis received considerable coverage in the media that fall, but once winter came the whole affair was forgotten. It burst forth again the following summer and lasted through the fall of 2000, especially at the Burnt Church First Nation. However, the media did not do a more extended analysis of the recurring nature of the crisis, nor did they put it in the context of the Mi'kmaq fishery as a whole, in New Brunswick and other provinces. The way these events were treated made the Burnt Church Mi'kmaq seem like Indians with whom it was impossible to reach an agreement. There was no understanding of their motives or the real reasons why negotiations between the Mi'kmaq and federal representatives had failed.

From there, it was only a short leap to the conclusion that these events were typical of the general attitude of Mi'kmaq in New Brunswick and, by extension, in Quebec and Nova Scotia. From the beginning of the crisis in 1999, at no time was a clear sense given of the significance of the difference between the amount of lobster demanded by the Mi'kmaq and the amount that Ottawa sought to impose on them in the name of conserving the resource. The gap between the two parties' figures was widely mentioned, but experts in the lobster fishery were not consulted in an effort to understand what these figures represented in terms of resource conservation. These are determining elements in an explanation of the conflict; when they are not dealt with, the effect is to prejudice public opinion rather than to inform it.

The situation of Aboriginal people in Canada is much more complex than the image we receive from the media. But even this simplified image carries with it a wealth of instruction. One of the perhaps unintended effects of the increased media coverage is that it has cast a harsh light on the policies that have been carried out towards Aboriginals for centuries. Because Aboriginal communities have been living under government guardianship for a long time, the question of how this system could have led to all these problems inevitably arises. To what extent have the problems been caused by the system that was set up to manage these communities, their members and their property? Recognition that the system has failed cannot be avoided any more, and this recognition challenges all of Canadian society. Pointing out that Aboriginal people have problems is no longer enough. All of society is faced with the need to acknowledge the failure of the system that it has established for Aboriginal people and to resolve the major problems engendered by this system.

Aboriginal people have suddenly become visible on the public stage. The narrow view of these questions that has led the public to believe that Aboriginal people are synonymous with problems is no longer satisfactory. Beyond the media imperative of ratings, we need to ask why we don't get more extensive information about other aspects of Aboriginal reality. The picture we get serves to hide problems that are just as serious but are not dealt with in the media, including the problem that currently poses the greatest challenge to Canadian society. The overall situation of Aboriginal people at the beginning of the twenty-first century proves that the system that has been imposed on them has failed. All across the country, socioeconomic indicators sketch a gloomy picture of the general condition of Indians in relation to the situation of other Canadian citizens.

The consequences of the status quo

If the current situation continues, it could have harmful consequences for Canadian society as a whole. Maintaining the status quo will result in faster deterioration of the overall situation of Aboriginal people and relations between them and other citizens. Persistence of the status quo will end up demonstrating that the special rights for Aboriginal peoples that were supposedly recognized when they were entrenched in the constitution in 1982 were in fact empty. The government cannot indefinitely use rhetoric that appears to indicate a willingness to change the foundations of Aboriginal people's status in Canada but has not led to any essential change in its treatment of Aboriginal questions. This rhetoric will have to be followed up with decisions, or the political option that took shape in 1982 will be a dead letter. If this happens, one consequence will be an increase in the already considerable frustration among Aboriginal people with regard to a political process that has left them hanging since the talks that led to the Meech Lake Accord in 1987. It is important not to give extremist elements in Aboriginal communities the opportunity to convince other members of those communities that the Canadian political process does not offer a real possibility of responding to their concerns. Our incapacity to bring issues that are essential to the future of Aboriginal people to the centre of political action and discussion will only help build the credibility of these disruptive elements.

We should not think that Aboriginal people will be satisfied with a theoretical recognition of their rights that is not followed up with legislative and administrative changes. We need to realize that the choice made in 1982 puts Aboriginal questions in a new perspective that represents a 180-degree turn from the Canadian policies that were applied for centuries. Such a radical change indicates that the status quo is not viable. Only measures that are clearly different will do. We cannot say that there are Aboriginal peoples in Canada and at the same time continue to treat Indians and Inuit as minors under federal guardianship. There is a flagrant contradiction here that will have to be resolved sooner or later. Otherwise, the existence of Aboriginal peoples will continue to be an empty shell, with no relation to the daily reality of Aboriginal communities.

Since 1995, the federal government has claimed to recognize that an inherent Aboriginal right to self-government has existed since 1982. This, too, is difficult to reconcile with the status quo. The idea of an inherent right was the stumbling block in the constitutional negotiations with Aboriginal people, who did not succeed in gaining acceptance for the idea that the rights recognized in 1982 included the right to govern themselves according to their own rules. Currently, the inherent right to self-government is recognized, but this right can be applied only if its exercise is circumscribed by an agreement, in a framework defined by Ottawa. A right that can be applied only if an agreement on its content is reached with the federal government is closer to a conditional right than an inherent right. At best, there is confusion in the terms being used. The risk is that the appearance of recognizing a principle that meets the concerns of Aboriginal people will raise great hopes, although this principle will not be put into effect. In the public mind, Aboriginals will still not be satisfied even though Ottawa is acquiescing to their demands, and people will take comfort in the generally accepted idea that nothing will satisfy them.

Maintaining the status quo also contributes to the disintegration of Aboriginal communities. This is catastrophic not only for Aboriginal people themselves but also for society as a whole, which will have to absorb the increasingly high costs of this situation. In light of the poor results obtained in exchange for the $6 billion Ottawa allocates annually for Aboriginal programs, the pertinence of such a system needs to be seriously questioned. Even taking account of the fact that these programs are not directed at all Aboriginal needs, their results have been extremely meagre in relation to the sums that have been spent annually for decades. Aboriginal people have suffered under the worst socioeconomic conditions in the country for a long time. In the current state of things, these conditions are unlikely to improve despite the increased expenditures directed at them.

Another look needs to be taken at this system. The gradual deterioration of the social fabric in Aboriginal communities will require increasing investment in social support policies in addition to development expenditures. If these communities become too fragile, their development could be compromised as well. If a feeling of collective abandonment were to settle in, the proactive members of Aboriginal communities might be unable to influence the course of events in a positive direction. It is in the interest of all of Canadian society to encourage Aboriginal people to heal the deep wounds caused by the past and, even more important, to commit themselves firmly to the difficult task of choosing a future that is appropriate for them.

Aboriginal people are the victims of a colonial past that we have still not willingly acknowledged. The current state of affairs may end up sapping their will to take charge of their own development, because they will be mobilized by the denunciation of a past that made them dependent on governments. We need to guard against increased dependence and put our trust in Aboriginals' collective capacity to take responsibility for their own situation, instead of allowing the continuation of a system whose failure can no longer be concealed.

[1] Canada, Department of Indian and Northern Affairs, *Statement of the Government of Canada on Indian Policy, 1969*, p. 3.

[2] Ibid., p. 5.

[3] Ibid., p. 5.

[4] Canada, Parliament, House of Commons, *Indian Self-Government in Canada: Report of the Special Committee*, p. 13.

[5] Ibid., p. 14.

[6] Canada, Royal Commission on Aboriginal Peoples, *Choosing Life: Special Report on Suicide among Aboriginal Peoples*, p. 38.

CHAPTER 2

Second-Class Status

L ooking at the many ways in which Aboriginal people have been marginalized throughout Canadian history, we can see clearly how they have consistently been given second-class status and begin to understand why they have refused to accept it. Before we explore the various aspects of their refusal, it makes sense first to define the nature of Aboriginal Canadians' assigned position. Examining the elements that characterize the special system set up for them will help us appreciate their current opposition.

From discovery to subjugation

Once the Europeans arrived in America, the indigenous nations were no longer the only players in the struggle for control of the continent, as they had been previously. We now know that in the pre-contact period the discovery of new land was consistently marked by conflict between indigenous groups throughout the American continent, even if our knowledge of the motivations and stakes in these conflicts remains incomplete. Indigenous societies had their own distinct languages and cultures, characterized in large part by activities defined by their geographic location. Some societies were made up of several nations, culturally similar although located quite far apart. Some of these developed into complex political and legal structures, eliminating smaller nations, absorbing them by force or forming alliances with them.

The arrival of the Europeans in America was a powerful blow to the development of an entire world. No doubt, idyllic depictions of this ancient world are not based in reality, but stem in part from recurring nostalgia for a paradise lost. There is enough evidence to show that even during the period when indigenous peoples had exclusive control over the land, before the European presence, the American continent was not immune from the struggles for power that have marked every period of human history all over the world. And yet, the chaos that the Europeans brought to this world when they arrived needs to be acknowledged. No one will ever know what changes Aboriginal societies would have undergone without European intervention in America. We cannot guess what might have happened; the only thing we can be sure of is that things would have been different.

We have a better understanding of the concept of world order as the European powers defined it at the time of the discoveries and during the centuries that followed. This concept was played out according to the interests of different European states, which fought over possession of the various lands they discovered all over the world, including the Americas. Initially, during an early period of exploration about which there is little historical documentation, Europeans came to America primarily to exploit the resources of the sea. They had little contact with the Aboriginal inhabitants of the continent, Indians and Inuit. This early exploration was succeeded by more organized and systematic efforts to establish a European presence.

From the moment that European rulers sent envoys to explore the unknown lands that would become the Americas, they expressed their overt intention to take control of these lands and to assert their authority over them. This would be the goal of numerous European expeditions, including those directed by England towards what is now Canada. The expeditions were searching for a route to the West, a search that would intensify from the fifteenth century on. Various documents, such as commissions, letters patent and royal instructions, attest to the colonial vision of the various European powers — England, Spain, France, Holland, Portugal and Sweden — that had claims in America. These documents frequently entrust the explorers with the task of subjugating, occupying and possessing the territories they discovered along with the buildings that were constructed there, in the name of a sovereign on whom the documents conferred authority over the territories. Thus were colonial regimes established throughout the Americas, founded on the principle that indigenous people were inferior beings whom one must bring to accept the virtues of civilization (that of the colonizers), which nature had not provided for them. The colonizers were incapable of recognizing any value in societies that functioned according to rules and systems unfamiliar to them; these were completely discredited in their eyes.

This approach formed the overall basis for the relationship that the French, the English and finally the Canadians would establish with Aboriginal peoples in Canada. A clear understanding of this historical reality is essential to an assessment of how much the colonial conception continues to affect the relationship between indigenous people and governments even now in the twenty-first century, in Canada and in most other countries that have indigenous populations. On the one hand, successive governments have viewed Aboriginals (both individuals and whole communities) as subject to their discretionary authority. For their part, the Aboriginals, Indians in particular, continue to resist being subjected to this form of supervision.

Historical sources: The European point of view

For more than five centuries, Europeans and their descendants have generally believed that historical documents expressing their view of the discovery of America and the relationships subsequently established with the indigenous peoples accurately reflected historical reality. Today, wherever they still have a presence, indigenous people are strongly contesting this Eurocentric interpretation and the documents supporting it. They criticize historians for having supported the notion that the European perspective represents all of history. Indigenous peoples do not see themselves reflected in a recounting of historical events that ignores them and supports European perspectives and interests alone. The mostly derogatory representation of Indians in history books offers eloquent testimony to the discredit in which historians have held them over the last five hundred years.

While the strangers who came to indigenous lands might have been acting in good faith, their relationships with the indigenous people were motivated primarily, if not exclusively, by European interests. Their version of these relationships, which has come down to us through historical documents, is a conqueror's version, based on commercial gains, colonization, strategic alliances and finally subjugation, carried out in several stages by various countries on the American continent.

This view of history has been largely endorsed by North American courts. The highest courts in both Canada and the United States have analyzed and interpreted colonial policies applied to the vast territory that the two countries inherited — the Supreme Court of Canada has often referred to United States Supreme Court decisions when interpreting such policies.

In the well-known 1832 case of *Worcester v. Georgia*, Chief Justice John Marshall of the U.S. Supreme Court defined the court's position in relation to European exploration and settlement of the American continent. This decision, which would form the basis for American and Canadian jurisprudence through the nineteenth and twentieth centuries, established that the great European maritime powers had, more or less simultaneously (starting in the fifteenth century), discovered and explored different parts of the American continent. None of these powers was able to take over the entire continent, but each was strong enough to avoid submitting to a single authority.

To prevent conflicts that would be destructive to all involved, the European countries needed to establish some principle that would determine their respective rights and be accepted by all. The principle they agreed on was actually no more than a statement of common practice at the time: Discovery of a territory conferred title on the country in whose name the discovery was made, as opposed to any other European power. This title would be confirmed by possession of the territory in question. According to the judge, it was in the interest of all the European nations to accept the principle that gave any country that discovered a territory exclusive rights to control and settle it.

And in practice this is what they did.

While it prevented conflicts between the powers that recognized it, this principle could not cancel the rights of those who had not agreed to it. It managed the right of discovery among the European powers, but it could not touch the rights of the indigenous or other previous occupants who already possessed the land. The principle gave the "discovering" state an exclusive right to buy the land, so that no other European power could intervene between the discovering state and the indigenous inhabitants, but it could not deny the owner's right to sell the land.

The rights of indigenous people were not totally eliminated, but they were substantially diminished. Indigenous people were considered the actual occupants of the land, with legal title of possession and use, which they could keep at their discretion. But their right to full sovereignty as independent nations was necessarily reduced. Further, their right to use the land as they wished was nullified by the principle of discovery, which gave exclusive ownership to the European power in whose name discovery had been made. In addition, governments had full power to extinguish indigenous nations' right to occupation — by treaty, by force, by purchasing the right, by the exercise of sovereignty or otherwise. The courts, meanwhile, concluded that they did not have the power to review such an extinguishment, nor could they comment on whether it was just or unjust.

This judicial opinion formed the basis for other court decisions in both the United States and Canada. It was completely based on the European interpretation of events. Lacking the political power of the European nations, Aboriginal nations did not hold any title of sovereignty or ownership to the lands they occupied that could be opposed to the European powers' claims. They could only maintain their rights to possession, which the various European countries that came to America sometimes recognized and at other times denied.

The legal principles applied were based on a theory put forth by many sixteenth-century lawyers, including Juan Ginès Sepulveda of Spain. According to him, the Indians of the New World were barbarians who worshiped stones and were by nature destined to be slaves. Although contested by a minority of lawyers, such as Bartolomé de Las Casas, Grotius and Vattel, the theory of the intrinsic inferiority of indigenous people prevailed, primarily because it reinforced the Europeans in the historical and legal theories that supported their interests.

The interpretation formulated by Justice Marshall in 1832 was adopted in Canada in several instances. In 1888, the judicial committee of the Privy Council in London, acting in its role as court of appeal for decisions rendered by the Supreme Court of Canada (an authority it maintained until 1949), rendered a similar judgement in the case of *St. Catherine's Milling & Lumber Co. v. R.* In its decision, Britain's highest court ruled that the defeat of Quebec in 1759, the capitulation of Montreal in 1760 and the transfer of Canada to Britain in 1763 conferred on Britain sovereignty, ownership, possession and all other rights over the territory that France had previously held. For the Privy Council, it was clear that title belonged to the ruling country, subject to an "Indian title," and that the title of the ruling country would become complete once Indian title had been ceded by the Aboriginal peoples or otherwise extinguished by the governing authorities.

This decision confirmed the power of the sovereign state to extinguish Indian title, either by voluntary cession or unilaterally — for example, by passing a law (with or without the consent of the Indians). Other litigation of this type also came before the Privy Council between 1880 and 1930. All of these cases concerned authority and rights of ownership over lands that Indians had ceded to the federal government. The Indians were not parties to these cases. Thus, the courts defined Indian title in the absence of principal interested parties. While the question has never been considered, this could explain in part why Indians view the Canadian judicial system as lacking in legitimacy. Fundamental issues concerning the nature and extent of the rights of Canadian Indians were decided on (as a side issue) by a British court during the late nineteenth and early twentieth centuries without their being able to intervene in the judicial process.

In the mid-twentieth century, the right to appeal to the judicial committee of the Privy Council was abolished, and the Supreme Court of Canada became the court of last resort. The Supreme Court adopted the same position as the Privy Council in many cases. Contemporary jurisprudence therefore continues to rely on the historical assumptions articulated by American courts, and Supreme Court of Canada decisions continue to refer to decisions made by the U.S. Supreme Court even though the Indian legal systems in the two countries are different. American influence was still prominent in a judgement made in 1973 that had serious repercussions. In *Calder,* a case brought by British Columbia Indians, a majority of Supreme Court justices, who held differing opinions about the core issue, nevertheless agreed on a fundamental point: The Indians who lived in America at the time the Europeans arrived formed nations and occupied the land as had their ancestors for centuries. They therefore held an "Indian title," based on the occupation and use of their traditional land, regardless of whether this right had been recognized by the powers that came after.

This decision marks an important break in Canadian jurisprudence from earlier decisions of the Privy Council, for which Indian title could not exist unless recognized by the state. For the first time, the highest court in the land ruled that the fact of occupation, whether recognized by the state or not, conferred legal title to those lands on Aboriginal people. On the other hand, the Supreme Court maintained the traditional position regarding the Indians' right of possession: This right existed subject to the supreme title of government, implying that the federal government could take away the right of possession.

Guardianship: An obstacle to Indians' development

It was not just Aboriginal title to the land that was subject to the power of governing authorities. Individual Aboriginals and whole communities were also put under government guardianship. There was continuity between the British colonial era (1760–1867) and the Confederation period (after 1867) as Canadian governments followed previous colonial, and especially British, policies. Not long after the Canadian federation was established, the federal Parliament, which has constitutional authority over "Indians, and lands reserved for the Indians" (article 91[24] of the British North America Act), consolidated various existing laws pertaining to Indians into one document. This system of governing Indians' lives, first codified in federal law in 1876, remains in effect today. It involves a system of guardianship over Aboriginal individuals and communities. The federal minister of the interior was clear when he introduced the bill: "The Indians must be treated like minors or like white men."[1]

In passing the bill, Parliament chose the first of the two solutions: Treat the Indians as minors, that is, wards of the state. The new act incorporated a number of regulations aimed at marginalizing traditional Aboriginal political structures that created obstacles to assimilation. Indians could have access to professions such as medicine, law or the priesthood only by voluntarily or involuntarily giving up their Indian status. By giving enfranchised Indians individual ownership of the areas they occupied on the reserve, the act ultimately brought about the extinction of the special communal character of Indian reserve lands and their incorporation into the provincial land tenure system. All of these measures had the effect of blocking Indian political, social and economic organization, to the point where it has become extremely complicated to try to change existing conditions.

While the Indian Act has been amended since its adoption more than 125 years ago, its basic principles have stayed the same. It defines the rules for Aboriginal individuals and communities, specifies the limits on local authority (the band council) and sets out the powers remaining with the federal government. Ottawa outlined the criteria that a person needs to meet to obtain Indian status and "created" what it calls bands — Indian communities recognized by the federal government, for whose use and profit the government has set aside lands known as "reserves." By virtue of this system, the federal government holds considerable power over the lives of individuals, Indian bands and reserves. Its powers are exercised either by cabinet or by the minister of Indian affairs. First, cabinet maintained the power of regulation within reserves in areas such as public security, road safety, health, wildlife resources and loans made by a band. The power to regulate loans means that the government can determine the conditions under which a band may borrow money. Furthermore, the Indian Act prohibits mortgages, securities and other guarantees of this sort, thus hindering community development. Indian communities can often obtain development funds only through designated programs established by Ottawa.

The government also retained the power to administer the land on Indian reserves. Only the government can create an Indian reserve. The government controls the extraction of natural resources on reserve lands, is the only body to which bands can cede their right of occupation and use of these lands, and holds the power to expropriate them. The government has also kept important powers related to the management of Indian communities. It can regulate areas such as the administration of justice within a band, band elections (including cancellation of elections), procedures for band council meetings and education. Finally, the government has the power to affect the lives of individuals, notably through the regulation of inheritance and the granting of loans.

Besides the powers the cabinet can exercise, others are available to the minister of Indian affairs. These include discretionary powers that give the minister a significant level of control over the management of internal community affairs. Thus, the minister can impose election rules on a community when he or she judges that it will improve administration of the band. For example, a band governed under customary rules regarding elections might have its rules set aside by ministerial decision. The minister can also cancel administrative rulings adopted by the band council in areas such as health and public safety, and decide whether or not to authorize the adoption of certain administrative regulations. A band council is subject to this right of preliminary authorization when the minister wishes to regulate such sectors of activity as property taxes, imposition of business taxes or allocation of funds for community expenses.

As the official responsible for managing Indian inheritances, the minister of Indian affairs can also intervene in the life of individuals. This responsibility gives the minister the discretionary power to annul an Indian's will if convinced that the clauses in the will are so "vague, uncertain or capricious" that they hamper proper administration and equitable distribution of the deceased person's goods.

As concerns the reserves, only the minister has the authority to grant rights to land on Indian reserves, first to Indians and Indian bands, and then to non-Aboriginals. As ownership of reserve lands belongs to the crown (the federal or provincial government), bands and individual Indians hold the right of ownership over lands on Indian reserves only in rare cases. The land is held by the government for the use and benefit of the communities for which it has been set aside. Individual Indians have at best a right of possession over a piece of land, which has to be granted by the band council with the approval of the minister of Indian affairs, who has sole authority to give a Certificate of Possession. In most cases, therefore, Indians have only a precarious right of occupation, granted by the band council, which can withdraw this right at will.

With respect to non-Aboriginals, only the minister has the authority to grant them permits or rights to land on a reserve. Any contract lasting up to a year can be authorized by the minister without approval by the band council. For a longer period, the council's consent is necessary. Thus, a contract, lease or any other form of agreement granting rights of occupation or use — hence, any lease agreement between an Indian and a non-Indian — is void if not signed by the minister. The minister is also responsible for managing a band's financial assets, both capital funds and revenues.

In addition to the cabinet and the minister of Indian affairs, the system governing reserves includes a third level of authority: the band council chief. Although the chief's status and functions are not clearly defined, he or she nevertheless acts as the political spokesperson for the community. The band council, which can be elected according to Indian custom or electoral procedures defined by law, constitutes the

political and administrative authority at the local level. It has the power
to govern the internal affairs of the community — but as we have seen,
much of this power is subject to significant control, both *a priori* and
a posteriori, by the federal government.

All the powers given to the government create a level of supervision
over individual Aboriginals and their communities that seriously compromises the integrity of their political structures and economic development and facilitates control of their social development. This
guardian-ward relationship represents a continuation of the attitude
displayed by earlier regimes, which saw these communities as needing
to be civilized by the imposition of modern rules of government.
Although these rules were foreign, they were seen as the only ones that
could produce a "high degree of advancement," regardless of whether
or not the communities were interested in their benefits.

Other measures only added to the effects of this guardianship
arrangement and confirmed Indians' second-class status. For example,
Indians were not allowed to vote until the second half of the twentieth
century (between 1949 and 1969), at either the federal or the provincial
level.

A fundamental right denied

Aboriginal people's relationship to the law has always been marked by
misunderstandings. One source of these misunderstandings has been
the difficulties they face in participating in legislative, administrative
and judicial institutions — in lawmaking, management of public life or
application and interpretation of the law through the courts.

In the Canadian system, legislation adopted by either level of government — federal or provincial — applies to all citizens. This principle is inscribed in the Canadian Charter of Rights and Freedoms,
adopted in 1982. Thus, a law applies to everyone unless it specifically
states otherwise. The courts are called on to adjudicate disputes and
apply the law, and among other things decide whether a transgression
committed by a citizen constitutes an infraction or crime punishable by

sanctions provided for in law.

In a democratic system, a law is an expression of the popular will, that is, it represents a social consensus about certain values enshrined in a legislative text. As representatives of the people, legislators are elected to express, in the name of the population, a consensus of values in various aspects and areas of life, which are then incorporated into legislation and become obligatory norms. Respect for the law is therefore based on citizens' voluntary adherence to norms outlined by elected representatives. The legitimacy of the law flows from the same principle. To the extent that laws reflect a social consensus, citizens made subject to them will tend to respect them. Laws also provide a basis for the courts to determine whether a particular behaviour is antisocial or transgresses a norm codified by law.

As we have seen, in the official view, the totality of legislative power, on both the legal and the political level, was divided in 1867 between the federal Parliament and the provincial legislative assemblies. In this view, no Aboriginal legislative jurisdiction survived the adoption of the Canadian constitution in 1867, and Aboriginal people no longer had the capacity to adopt laws solely on their own authority.

It is important to remember that Aboriginal people did not have the right to vote in federal elections until 1960, nearly a century after Confederation. Many provinces also passed laws denying Aboriginals the right to vote in provincial elections. This continued until 1949 when British Columbia became the first province to reestablish the right to vote. It was not until 1969 that Quebec, the last province to revive voting rights, allowed Indians living on reserves to vote at the provincial level.

At the federal level, while Indians were generally deprived of the right to vote until 1960, various laws were adopted from 1885 on specifying exceptions under certain conditions. For example, federal laws passed in 1917 and 1944 gave the right to vote to Indian members of the Canadian armed forces who had fought in the two world wars. In some cases, the conditions for gaining the right to vote brought heavy consequences, such as giving up Indian status, treaty rights or tax exemptions on personal assets and real estate. The Inuit were denied the right to vote in federal elections by a law passed in 1934. They regained it in 1950, but were not able to exercise it until 1962 when ballot boxes were finally brought to their communities. It is also worth noting that Inuit could not benefit from the rule applied to Indians who were members of the armed forces.

Legislators invoked various arguments between 1867 and 1960 to justify their decision to deny Aboriginal people the right to vote. These included their status as wards of the state, the lack of education among Indians, the risk that they would be manipulated by the government in exercising their franchise, the distinct legal status of Indians, the tax exemptions Indians enjoyed, the reserve system (under which Indian bands and individuals could not own land since the reserves belong to the state) and even the political awakening of the Aboriginal population. This situation later led a committee of federal Aboriginal parliamentarians to say that Ottawa had used the right to vote as a tool of assimilation, and that this had engendered a great deal of Aboriginal mistrust of Parliament.

Inspired by the work of this committee, the Royal Commission on Electoral Reform recommended in 1992 that the Canadian electoral system be changed so as to guarantee direct representation of Aboriginals in Parliament. This would be accomplished by creating electoral districts specially reserved for Aboriginals. The recommendation was not implemented. In this context, it is not surprising to note that turnout by Aboriginal voters has always been relatively low in federal elections and generally even lower in provincial elections. Aboriginal chiefs have at times called on members of their communities to boycott elections.

The right to vote is a fundamental democratic right. It underpins a system in which the elected governing body can make laws to which citizens will be subject and the courts can impose sanctions on those who do not obey these laws. In this country, we seek to apply laws to Aboriginal people knowing that we long deprived them of the right to have a say in electing representatives to our federal and provincial legislative institutions. This inevitably raises questions of legitimacy: of these institutions as expressions of the values of Aboriginal people, and of the rules that they adopted when Aboriginals had no chance to express their point of view. These questions have increasingly come to the fore in Aboriginal communities since the 1960s. They are claiming their inherent right to govern themselves according to their own rules, separate from a seat of legislative power that excluded them for a century and is of dubious legitimacy in their eyes.

White justice for Aboriginal people

After questioning the legitimacy of the law, the next step for Aboriginal people is to question the credibility of the component of the state that is responsible for administering justice and applying the law — the courts. How can the system applying the laws, whose legitimacy is already tainted, be considered legitimate by Aboriginal people? How can the courts, whose judges are appointed by the government that creates the laws, hold more legitimacy than the laws that they apply? It is useful to distinguish here between the period before repatriation of the Canadian constitution in 1982 and the post–1982 period.

Before 1982, it was very difficult for Aboriginal people to win cases in which they invoked ancestral rights to land they had traditionally occupied, especially in parts of Canada where they had not signed treaties in exchange for giving up their rights. The courts did not recognize the special rights of Aboriginals as the first inhabitants of America. They only recognized those rights that they had been expressly granted.

Indians signed historic treaties in exchange for their ancestral rights across a broad swath of Canadian territory stretching from the eastern boundary of Ontario to the western boundary of Alberta. In the rest of the country — the territories (Yukon, Northwest Territories and now Nunavut), the Atlantic provinces (Prince Edward Island, New Brunswick, Nova Scotia and Newfoundland), Quebec and British Columbia — there were no such treaties, since the French were regarded as having already extinguished Aboriginals' rights before the British conquest in 1760. On this basis, the courts refused to recognize any Aboriginal ancestral rights until the 1973 decision in the *Calder* case.

Before 1982, Canadian courts were generally inclined to interpret legislation strictly, on the theory that defining Aboriginal rights was the responsibility of legislators and not the courts. Since 1982, the situation has changed dramatically. Repatriation of the Canadian constitution marks an important moment in the recognition of Aboriginal rights in Canada. For the first time, Canada expressly recognized Aboriginals' rights in a constitutional document. Their ancestral rights and their rights flowing from treaties are now confirmed. In addition, the constitution recognizes Aboriginal peoples as peoples. It distinguishes three Aboriginal peoples in Canada: Indians, Inuit and Métis.

Constitutionally protected rights override federal and provincial law. This means that laws cannot diminish these rights. At the very least, governments must now justify any legislative attack on these rights on the basis of criteria that the Supreme Court of Canada began to define after 1982. If the government cannot justify its legislation, the rights will prevail and the legislation will not apply to Aboriginals. For example, in the *Marshall* case, which was front-page news in the fall of 1999, the Supreme Court decided that the federal Fisheries Act did not apply to the Mi'kmaq Indians of New Brunswick. The decision was based on Ottawa's failure even to try to explain why its legislation was necessary and should override fishing rights guaranteed to the Mi'kmaq in a treaty signed in 1760. As the Mi'kmaq fishing rights are constitutionally protected, they take precedence over the federal act interfering with those rights, given that the government did not demonstrate any valid reason for limiting them. Ottawa could have tried to justify the act, and it is impossible to know what the court would have decided if it had.

The legal situation for Aboriginals therefore changed completely in 1982. The new constitutional provisions provided a much more solid legal basis for Aboriginals' claims. They therefore increased efforts to have their rights recognized by Canadians in general, by legislators and by the courts. With the basis for Aboriginal rights now entrenched in the constitution, the attitude of the courts had to change too, and this is exactly what happened after 1982. In addition, the Supreme Court chose to adopt, in its own words, a "generous, liberal interpretation" of the Aboriginal rights recognized in 1982, in consideration of the poor treatment Aboriginals had received historically and the government's obligations towards them.

This constitutional recognition of their rights does not seem to have influenced Aboriginals' attitudes towards the law in general, which they still treat as something that does not concern them. Fear of sanctions attached to breaking the law apparently does not serve as a motivation to obey it. This is one reason that Aboriginals have a tendency to plead guilty to charges brought for summary infractions and even criminal offenses. For example, in the area of wildlife conservation, when facing charges relating to activities such as hunting or fishing without a permit, hunting migratory birds out of season, harvesting the eggs of migratory birds or fishing with nets, they do not deny the activities, but argue that they are allowed to pursue these activities, which are permitted within their own code of values.

The legal process was not designed to adapt to the particular reality of Aboriginal people or even take them into account. When the first laws regulating Indians were adopted, the administration of justice was entrusted to federal bureaucrats, who fulfilled judicial as well as administrative functions. This put them in a conflict of interest, as the same person would receive the complaint, lay the charges and act as judge in the case. Such a system has created deep mistrust of the administration of justice among Aboriginals.

In addition to the conflict of values and the imposition of a foreign system, the language barrier has been another obstacle that continues even today to cause misunderstandings. An Aboriginal who knows neither English nor French (the two official languages in Canadian courts) is dependent on an interpreter in addition to a lawyer (possibly a legal aid lawyer who travels with an itinerant court in remote areas) with whom he or she may not have had the time or opportunity to establish even a minimal level of trust. Furthermore, interpreters do not always have the necessary training for their specific role in the judicial system or sufficient knowledge of the consequences of various oaths and other testimony by the accused in court.

During a trial, the judge and the lawyers for both sides are no less dependent on the interpreter than the accused. As these players would not usually be familiar with the language of the accused, they are not in a position to assess the skill of the interpreter or evaluate any possible pressure on the accused from the community. Adequate training for all those involved in a trial is essential so that the individuals and the process itself will be at least minimally credible. There have been a variety of initiatives to establish new Aboriginal paralegal services. Aboriginal paralegals are supposed to give basic information to the accused about the nature of the infraction or the criminal act attributed to them and ensure that they at least understand the basic steps in the process and the consequences. It should not be imagined, however, that this will be enough to increase the credibility of the legal process. All those involved — and particularly the non-Aboriginals, who are generally the authority figures in this process — must be trained to deal with the particular context involved. Such training must focus both on the special rights of Aboriginals in the Canadian legal system and on the values and specific rules of different Aboriginal communities.

For Aboriginal people, the judicial system and its players appear to be tools of a state that does not recognize their rights. Whether justified or not, this perception translates into the sentiment among Aboriginal communities that collaborating with the judicial apparatus (at least in the area of criminal law) means joining forces with the enemy. As a result, many people put up with problems in their communities rather than risk having one of their own condemned by a justice system perceived as foreign. Such an attitude remains prevalent in many Aboriginal communities.

Indians are also increasingly challenging the authority of the courts that are called on to judge them and deal with cases concerning their rights. They frequently invoke rights of full sovereignty and ownership over their traditional lands, arguing that as a result the Canadian constitution does not apply to them. This approach challenges the very sovereignty of the state and its ownership of all Canadian territory. The scope of the discussion engendered by the land claims currently being made by various Aboriginal groups is thus extremely broad.

Indians also invoke the right to make their own laws and apply them in their own courts. This position, which they expressed in the constitutional conferences held between 1983 and 1987 and have repeated since, would see a third order of government enshrined in the constitution, an Aboriginal order with its own powers parallel to the federal and provincial governments. The conflicts that arose around lobster fishing by the Burnt Church Mi'kmaq once again demonstrated Aboriginal mistrust of the judicial system. The media reported that when the Mi'kmaq accused of illegal lobster fishing appeared in court, some of them began to exchange words with the judge, challenging the authority of Canadian judges to determine Indians' rights.

Non-Aboriginal lawyers who represent Aboriginals find themselves in a novel position. At the very least, they can easily appear to be an extension of the "white" justice system. There is a perception that a kind of non-Aboriginal solidarity will surface sooner or later: Forced to choose, a non-Aboriginal lawyer will line up on the side of his or her own society rather than the client's. Well founded or not, this perception plays a role above and beyond the considerations ostensibly being discussed in the case. The level of suspicion may soften, but it will likely never disappear. This mistrust becomes even more of an issue when the lawyer is a woman. How can Indians have confidence in a non-Indian woman, even if they recognize her technical competence, when women in many Aboriginal communities are excluded from debates on public issues? I have long noticed the irony in a situation where Indian political authorities seek advice from a non-Indian female lawyer and yet continue to believe that Aboriginal women have no place in political decision-making. Being plunged into a world where my usual references no longer serve as valid indicators has helped me better understand what it might mean for Aboriginals to have to submit to the

Canadian judicial system, a process that is foreign to them.

One might think that this phenomenon will dissipate as more Aboriginals become lawyers. However, another phenomenon is emerging. While Aboriginals will not hesitate to engage non-Aboriginal lawyers, who are familiar with the world in which they must defend themselves, they will often have doubts, which they sometimes clearly express, about the abilities of Aboriginal lawyers to represent them in this foreign world.

There is one area where the problem of the dubious legitimacy of legislation and the courts is especially acute: Indians do not benefit from the same protections against discrimination as other Canadian citizens. The rules governing Indians are excluded from the federal act that provides recourse in cases of discrimination. This is one of the least known aspects of the distinctly unfavourable treatment reserved for Indians in Canadian law.

The absence of recourse against discrimination

Indians do not have the same protection from discrimination as other Canadian citizens under federal law. This unique situation stems from the fact that when Parliament passed the Canadian Human Rights Act in 1978, it made one exception: It exempted the Indian Act and all that flows from it from the new act. Thus, Indians are the only group of people in Canada who cannot take advantage of the protection offered by the act. Even non-citizens who are legally in Canada seeking citizenship can benefit from this protection. This exclusion shows the extent to which Indians have been separated from the rest of Canadian society — not only historically, by regimes that no longer exist, but even by our contemporary Canadian political system.

During the parliamentary debates that preceded passage of the act, Justice Minister Ron Basford, speaking for the government, said that this exclusion was motivated by ongoing consultations with the Indians. He based this statement on the Indians' request that no amendment be made to the Indian Act without their consent. The minister's words seem to suggest that the government viewed this exclusion as temporary, and that it would end when consultations on the Indian Act concluded. These consultations had begun in the wake of the 1969 federal white paper, when Indians challenged Ottawa's desire to transfer its authority to the provinces.

The government knew that some aspects of the system provided for in the Indian Act were considered discriminatory, especially by Indian women. While the Supreme Court had invalidated clauses that banned possession of alcohol on Indian reserves because they contravened the Canadian Bill of Rights, it had declared another clause of the act valid in 1974, refusing to recognize discrimination against Indian women who lost their status by marrying non-Indians and therefore could not pass on status to their children. At the same time, Indian men who married non-Indians not only kept their status but also passed it on to their spouses and children.

Under this system, an Indian woman could lose her status through marriage while a non-Indian woman could gain Indian status through marriage. The Supreme Court did not find this discriminatory because it applied to all women equally. The court did not want to examine the question from the point of view that Indian women were disadvantaged in relation to Indian men. Even after the controversial Supreme Court decision, this aspect of the act continued to be widely criticized, and Indian women challenged it before the United Nations Commission on Human Rights, which ruled in their favour in 1981. The law was finally changed in 1985, but the change only partially corrected the discrimination against women.[2]

Discussions were initiated between the federal government and Indian representatives over possible changes to the system governing Indians. The government appears to have been in a hurry because of the likelihood that a court would invalidate several articles of the Indian Act as discriminatory under the new Human Rights Act. It is important to note that a number of Indian spokespeople clearly indicated that they were in favour of the provisions in the Indian Act that denied Indian status to women who marry non-Indian men. If there was one point on which the Indian representatives and Ottawa agreed, albeit for completely different reasons, it was this one: They were objective allies in maintaining the *status quo* to the detriment of women. The federal government did not want to see its system cut in pieces by the courts, while the Indian chiefs believed that this issue should come under their authority and not Ottawa's. The chiefs vigorously reaffirmed this position, most notably during the constitutional conference of 1983, which focused on equality of rights for Aboriginal men and women. The government's solution was to prevent the courts from dealing with such delicate issues, which it did through article 67 of the 1978 Human Rights Act.

The exception formulated in this article applies both to Indians and to people who are not Indians under the Indian Act: Neither an Indian nor a non-Indian can challenge the system. An Indian cannot complain of discrimination against him or her, while non-Indians cannot argue that the special status given Indians, such as exemption from taxes, constitutes discrimination against them. In addition, everything that flows from the act is excluded: regulations adopted by Ottawa or by a band council (the act allows band councils to adopt administrative regulations of a local nature) as well as all actions taken by the federal government and band councils under the Indian Act.

Thus, Indians as individuals do not have recourse when they feel they are victims of discrimination because of the effect of an article of the Indian Act or a regulation adopted by the government in accordance with that act. For example, the daughter of an Indian woman who married a non-Indian cannot challenge the provisions that give her more limited status than her cousin whose father is Indian. An Indian student living off-reserve cannot challenge a federal scholarship program that limits eligibility to Indians living on reserves.

Nor can an Indian contest the discriminatory aspect of an administrative regulation adopted by his or her band council, or any decision, program or activity of the band council that flows from the Indian Act. For example, a band member cannot challenge discrimination that comes from membership rules adopted by a band council in accordance with the act. Similarly, an Indian cannot contest a band council decision refusing him or her services such as education, health or lodging for discriminatory reasons.

It is not only individuals who are deprived of recourse in cases of discrimination; groups are excluded as well. A group of Indians, whether or not represented by their band council, has no recourse under Canadian law if they believe they are subject to discrimination resulting from a provision of the Indian Act, a regulation adopted in accordance with the act or a federal program or activity stemming from it. In addition, a group of Indians that would like to challenge discrimination arising from an administrative regulation adopted by a band council or a band council decision, program or activity flowing from the act is likewise deprived of any recourse under the Canadian Human Rights Act.

Furthermore, individuals and groups who are not considered Indians under the Indian Act cannot challenge the discriminatory aspects of the legislation. Thus, the Inuit have no opportunity to argue that the government's decision not to include them in the system set up for Indians, with its tax exemptions, constitutes discrimination against them. Similarly, non-Indians cannot challenge the special system for Indians on grounds that it discriminates against them and demand that it be abolished. Nor do these individuals and groups have an option when they feel they have suffered discrimination because of the effect of the act or because of a decision, program or activity of either the federal government or a band council. A number of different categories of people might wish to enter such a challenge: people who have no relation to the Indians, who might wish to challenge the tax exemptions provided for in the Indian Act; people who have a professional connection with Indians, such as non-Indian nurses or teachers hired by the government or a band council to work on an Indian reserve; people with a personal connection to Indians, such as a non-Indian spouse or child of an Indian; or perhaps someone of Indian ancestry who does not meet all the criteria under the act or under a band council's membership rules and who believes that the criteria are discriminatory.

When ruling on this aspect of the Canadian Human Rights Act, the courts have interpreted the exclusion of Indians strictly. This narrow interpretation of article 67 was based on a recognition of the special character of this act, which is designed to ensure the protection of fundamental rights. Thus, a band council's refusal to provide services to a man who was raised in the Mohawk community according to its culture and language on the grounds that he is not 50 per cent Mohawk by blood was ruled discriminatory. On the other hand, the court held that article 67 sheltered certain other activities of this band council from the act because acceptance of its electoral rules by the minister of Indian affairs put them outside the courts' jurisdiction.

Even after the Canadian constitution recognized that the Indians, Inuit and Métis together constitute the "Aboriginal peoples," and that as such they hold certain collective rights, including ancestral rights and treaty rights, the federal government and the band councils continue to be sheltered from any legal action based on discrimination stemming from the special legal system created by the Indian Act. Neither an individual nor a group, Indian or non-Indian, can bring such action. In the context of this exclusion, there is no motivation for Ottawa to amend the Indian Act to make it conform to the Canadian Human Rights Act, especially since the exclusion, not well known to the public, has never been the object of a campaign for abolition, except by Indian women. Abrogation of the exclusion of Indians from the Canadian Human Rights Act should be accompanied by changes in federal policies — dealing with land claims and Aboriginal self-government, among other matters — so that agreements reached with band councils and tribal councils would provide for appropriate mechanisms to protect band members' fundamental rights.

Band councils should also revise their internal regulations and management to eliminate any discriminatory aspects and add protection mechanisms for the fundamental rights of the people they serve. The new internal regulations would stem from current powers held by the councils or powers provided for in treaties, land claims agreements or self-government agreements. All agreements, on whatever basis, should include provisions dealing with the protection of fundamental rights. Internal regulations should also ensure the protection of Indians and non-Indians who have a professional or personal relationship with Indians in the community. In addition, while they could provide explicitly for the protection, promotion and development of the culture of the Indian community involved, they should also guarantee equality of rights between men and women.

Displacement of Aboriginal communities

Since the Europeans first arrived in America, Aboriginal people have been increasingly relegated to a space and a place in society where their status was not quite the same as that of other citizens. Prime Minister Pierre Elliott Trudeau recognized this in a speech he gave in Vancouver in 1969. Trudeau stated that Canadians had nothing to be proud of in the way they had treated Canadian Indians, whom they had isolated from society and made a separate "race." According to the prime minister, the country was at a crossroads. It could choose further discrimination, continuing to keep Aboriginal people in the "ghetto"[3] in which they lived, which would probably have the effect of helping them preserve certain cultural traits and ancestral rights. Alternatively, it could make them full-fledged citizens. It is interesting to note that Trudeau clearly understood that the current system has a dual character: It is discriminatory, which is why there are more and more protests attacking it, and it reinforces Indians' distinct cultural identity, which runs counter to government policies that refuse to recognize Indian ancestral rights.

The assessment that Trudeau made in his 1969 speech can also be applied to another little-known aspect of the differential treatment that Aboriginal people have received. It involves actions that, throughout the twentieth century, destabilized a large number of Aboriginal communities, both Indian and Inuit. Up to now, we have not taken the full measure of the effects of government decisions, which quite often were disastrous for Aboriginal communities in Canada. Some of these decisions had serious repercussions, and we are only now beginning to see the harmful long-term consequences that have resulted. I am referring to the displacement of Aboriginal populations — forced, or for dubious reasons, or carried out under false representations when the move was ostensibly voluntary.

The displacement of a population can be forced or voluntary. It can be the work of a state or the result of a collective movement for survival. It can happen in various situations, in times of peace or war, and can be undertaken for political, strategic or administrative reasons. In the twenty-first century, it is difficult not to be aware of the harmful effects of moving an entire population. Media images of long lines of displaced persons resulting from the many conflicts that took place in the world during the twentieth century illustrate the individual and collective tragedies caused by these wholesale population movements.

It is not generally known that Canada pursued a policy of Aboriginal population transfer during the twentieth century. And yet, who does not remember the images of the tragic situation of an Innu Indian community in Labrador, shown on television throughout the world in the late 1990s? Since then, it has been difficult to associate the name Davis Inlet with anything other than the scenes of individual and collective despair expressed in those images. What the images did not reveal, however, was that this community had been the object of several relocations during the second half of the twentieth century.

The federal government's relocation policy can be seen as a continuation of the colonization policies of centuries past. The underlying pattern has not changed. Aboriginal people are frequently moved to satisfy the needs of development or to facilitate government administration; they are rarely moved on their own request. A number of motives are generally cited: to ensure better services for Aboriginals, to protect them from game shortages or diseases, even to bring them close to a city where they can become wage-earners. In contrast to the earlier policy of keeping Aboriginal people away from large urban centres, from the 1950s on, Ottawa seemed to want to bring them closer to areas populated by non-Aboriginals, where they could more easily find paid work.

Population transfer took place all over Canada, from Yukon through almost every Canadian province to Labrador. In some cases, the transfers took place against the express will of the Aboriginals. In other cases, their formal consent was obtained, although a number of the groups that were moved argue that the real conditions of the move and resettlement were not explained. In every case, the Aboriginal group's agreement or disagreement was not a determining factor, as the decision had already been made by the authorities. Ironically, these transfers produced the opposite effect from the one the government sought: The displaced Aboriginal communities became more and more dependent on government subsidies.

Some operations, such as the displacement of the Nova Scotia Mi'kmaq in the 1940s, consisted of bringing together dispersed members of the same nation. Approximately twenty Mi'kmaq communities were forced to regroup in two reserves designated by Ottawa. This "centralization," imposed for reasons of administrative convenience, led to problems in relations between the new arrivals and the host communities, which had not been consulted about the move. The two reserves were cramped and services were deficient. The resulting overpopulation engendered significant social problems, especially since the prospects of economic development tied to agriculture did not work out in practice, as even government representatives acknowledged. Protests emanated both from Indians who did not want to leave their home reserves and from the communities called on to receive the "displaced." Even bureaucrats eventually doubted the government's genuine desire to take the necessary steps to bring this massive "experiment" to a conclusion. Lack of housing, contaminated water, absence of game and the refusal of several groups to leave their original reserves were just a few of the factors that made the experiment a total failure.

At the same time, Ottawa also went ahead with other operations on a smaller scale. For example, the Montagnais Indians of Pakuashipi lived near the mouth of the Saint-Augustin River on the lower North Shore of Quebec in the summer and moved all over northeastern Quebec and Labrador during the rest of the year. In the 1960s these

Indians still lived in tents and did not receive any services worth mentioning from the federal government. Ottawa had refused to set up a reserve and build a permanent village with houses at Saint-Augustin for this community, which it considered too small. The minister of Indian affairs decided instead to move the hundred or so Pakuashipi Montagnais to La Romaine, where another Montagnais community lived on a reserve. It was not until the Pakuashipi Montagnais returned home on foot with their goods that the minister finally agreed to set them up in Saint-Augustin.

Some displacements were directly linked to the activities of corporations such as the Hudson's Bay Company, which in its fur-trading operations had established trading posts that moved periodically as animal migration patterns changed and that were finally closed during the second half of the twentieth century. The population transfers were thus planned by government authorities in concert with the primary actors: resource-extraction companies and missionary authorities established in Aboriginal communities.

The underlying motives for displacing Aboriginal populations were also tied to the desire to develop new territories and natural resources. Hydroelectric, oil and gas, mining and other development projects were often behind these operations. So it was that the Saugeen Ojibwa Indians of southern Ontario, despite a promise that there would be no further encroachment on their lands, were forcibly relocated several times during the nineteenth century to advance settlement and agricultural development. In British Columbia, the Songhee Indians were moved from the reserve that they occupied in Victoria in the early twentieth century. Their presence in the city seems to have been the object of numerous complaints from non-Aboriginals from the mid-nineteenth century on. The federal and provincial governments agreed, in 1910, to move the Songhees from this extremely valuable land so that the port of Victoria could be enlarged.

In the same province, construction of a hydroelectric station and dam in the 1950s prompted the dislocation of the Cheslatta Indians, who occupied ten reserves. The Aluminum Company of Canada

(Alcan) was behind the project, which required flooding the land on which the reserves were located. Members of the band have argued that the consent the Cheslatta gave to the move was not valid, because it was obtained in a very short period of time and through an election organized for that purpose. In the end, the flooding did not take place as quickly as expected, so the haste does not appear to have been necessary. In addition, the Cheslatta faced very difficult conditions in the place to which they were relocated, where they lived in tents, suffered from a variety of diseases and did not receive the compensation, housing and land they were promised. Some of them lived in such destitution that they were moved once again, dispersed to areas far away from their original land and other Cheslatta communities. This case finally culminated in a deal between the Cheslatta and the federal government in 1993, involving a payment of more than $7 million in compensation. The amount reflected the 1993 value of the sum that the band understood it should have received back in 1952 along with payment for a church and damage to Cheslatta cemeteries washed away by the floods resulting from the project.

In Manitoba, the Grand Rapids hydroelectric project, begun in the late 1950s, led to the relocation of Cree Indians and Métis communities in 1964 because of the flooding of land occupied by some Cree bands. The Indians received a letter of intent from the government of Manitoba in 1960, advising them that they would have to leave their traditional lands, which would be flooded as a result of the project. The federal government had previously tried to incorporate the Chemawawin Crees into another group to get them to move when Treaty No. 5 was signed in 1875, which they refused to do. In the 1960s they were promised infrastructure and services (such as a "semi-modern" dispensary) that led them to accept the move to an urban site with access roads and modern installations. As a result of several factors, including a decrease in game in the region, the Crees became increasingly dependent on the government.

Until the late 1990s, Canadians were not fully informed of the reality of population transfers, which explains the current level of ignorance about the consequences of these moves. Various organizations representing Aboriginal people tried to make Canadians aware of the harmful effects these policies had on their communities. With few exceptions, their protests and pressure, recorded in government archives, did not yield results. It was not until the 1990s that they would succeed in attracting the attention of some institutions to what they considered unresolved injustices.

The Canadian Human Rights Commission called inquiries into two population moves carried out in the mid-twentieth century: the relocation of the Mushuau Innu within Labrador (Newfoundland) and that of the Inuit of Quebec and the Northwest Territories to the eastern Arctic. These inquiries were initiated in response to complaints brought by the Indian and Inuit groups involved, who maintained that these relocations constituted discrimination against them by the government of Canada.

In a report on the situation of the Mushuau Innu of Labrador released in 1993, an independent investigator hired by the Human Rights Commission came to the conclusion that the repeated displacement of these Indians was a violation of their fundamental rights. The investigator concluded that the federal government had not assumed its responsibilities towards the Mushuau Innu after Newfoundland joined Confederation as a province in 1949 and had done nothing to prevent them from being displaced for reasons totally unrelated to their interests.

Newfoundland provincial authorities displaced the Mushuau Innu because of the closing of a store, and again because the government wanted to transform these Indians into fishers when they had always been hunters. In one case, it carried out the displacement without formally consulting them, and in the other by making them promises that never materialized. These moves were carried out in 1948, when Newfoundland was not yet part of Canada, and again in 1967, well after its entry into Confederation. According to the investigator, Ottawa's negligence in failing to correct the untenable situation created by the 1967 move rendered it directly responsible for the acute social crisis that the community is experiencing today. In fact, the Labrador Innu have found themselves in administrative limbo. On one hand, federal authorities neglected to offer them constitutionally mandated services provided to Indians elsewhere in Canada. On the other hand, Newfoundland provincial authorities took the position that they did not have to pay for services provided to Aboriginal populations living in the province, especially since the 1949 Terms of Union did not mention these costs. The investigator also found that Ottawa's refusal to recognize the Mushuau Innu's Indian status and provide them with services flowing from that status constituted discrimination.

In this case, as in other cases of population transfer, one of the premises of the operation, according to the investigator, was the belief that the Innu should become white. According to him, Innu complaints and protests were not taken into consideration, and poor housing conditions (the absence of a drinking water supply system, the mediocre quality of the homes and the like) led to a deterioration in the mental and physical health of individuals, as well as a radical reduction in the quality of life of the community as a whole. Government authorities knew very well that the situation at Davis Inlet was critical. But they did not act until the media went public with brutal images of the crisis, the most obvious symptoms of which were extremely high rates of suicide, attempted suicide and drug use, even among very young children.

Three years after the inquiry report was published, the Royal Commission on Aboriginal Peoples reiterated some of the same elements in its final report, released in 1996. In its analysis of the federal policy of Aboriginal population transfer, the commission examined the case of the Mushuau Innu as a typical case of relocation that produced devastating effects on a community that had been moved for reasons of administrative convenience, under cover of humanitarian motives. It is no accident that the federal government reacted by making a public commitment to take steps to promote the economic development of the Mushuau in 1994, after the media had shown the urgency of the situation through images transmitted around the world and commentators had highlighted the shocking nature of the situation.

New and equally shocking images appeared in the media during the fall of 2000, showing several dozen children intoxicated by gas fumes and living abandoned in the woods on the outskirts of the village. These images have forced us to realize that the efforts that have so far been agreed on have not been enough to stop the continuing deterioration of living conditions for this Indian community in Labrador, and that massive investments in human and financial resources will be required.

In the 1990s the Canadian Human Rights Commission also hired an independent investigator to deal with complaints filed by political authorities representing the Inuit regarding the transplantation of Inuit from northern Quebec and the Northwest Territories to the High Arctic. In 1991, the investigator's report concluded that the federal government had not respected its obligations to Aboriginal people in the planning and execution of this relocation project. It had refused to take the necessary steps to allow those who wished to go back to their villages of origin to do so, contrary to the agreement it had made with the displaced Inuit. The report also highlighted the suffering, directly caused by the lack of organization and planning, that the Inuit endured during the displacement. These hardships were experienced not only by those who were moved but also by their descendants and the many families that were separated by the operation. For this reason, the investigator recommended that the government apologize to the Inuit for these operations and take a number of measures to alleviate their devastating effects, including paying the costs of relocation for those who wished to go back.

The Royal Commission on Aboriginal Peoples' research into the unknown reality of the relocation of Aboriginal people in Canada led it to conclude that the federal government had pursued a policy of displacement, by force or through its own decision, over many years and for a variety of reasons. At the request of the Inuit, the commission also agreed to study the situation of displaced Inuit in the High Arctic, and it produced a special report on the resettlement operations of 1953–55. The commission learned about this problem, which the Inuit said was unresolved, during the series of regular public hearings it held across Canada in 1992. It then decided to hold special public hearings in Ottawa in 1993.

The federal government conducted the removal operation in two parts. The first relocation took place in 1953, when seven Inuit families from northern Quebec and three from the Northwest Territories, fifty people in all, were brought to Craig Harbour on Ellesmere Island and Resolute on Cornwallis Island in the Canadian Arctic. A second relocation was conducted in 1955. Forty people, members of four Inuit families from Quebec and two from the Northwest Territories, joined the families that had been moved two years earlier. The Inuit at Resolute were eventually joined by two more families from Quebec and one from the Northwest Territories. The government gave up its original idea of placing these families in a third "colony" on the east coast of Ellesmere Island opposite Greenland when the boat carrying them was unable to reach its destination because of bad weather.

It is important to put this operation in the legal context of the period. The Supreme Court of Canada had forced the federal government to ensure the provision of public services to the Inuit beginning in 1939. However, Ottawa did not want to extend the Indian reserve system to the Inuit, and so in 1951 it specified that the Indian Act did not apply to the Inuit. A bill aimed at subjecting the Inuit to this act, introduced in 1924, had been withdrawn following protests from the opposition in the House of Commons, who argued that the proposal would reduce the Inuit to being wards of the state. This argument is a good illustration of the perception of the system put in place for Indians at the time.

From the time they arrived in the Arctic, the relocated Inuit protested the extremely harsh conditions that they faced, having neither the resources nor the equipment they needed to live in this new environment. They objected to the separation of families on arrival, which had not been announced, and to the government's refusal to bring them back home in spite of what they had been promised. It proved difficult for Inuit from Quebec and those from the Northwest

Territories to live together because of cultural differences. In addition, relocation had been presented to the families from the Northwest Territories as an initiative that would give them the opportunity to help the families from Quebec, who had been depicted as welfare recipients.

The Inuit always felt that they were there to shore up Canada's sovereignty in the Arctic, while the Canadian government insisted on the humanitarian nature of the relocations, as a solution to the disappearance of game and Inuit overpopulation in northern Quebec. Studies have examined this question over the years at the request of one party or the other, and they agree on two points. First, deficiencies in the planning and implementation of these relocations caused problems that affected not only the displaced Inuit but also their home communities and have left their mark even among the descendants of those involved. Second, the Canadian government did not keep certain promises that it had made to the displaced Inuit. This is probably what led it to sign a reconciliation agreement with the Inuit of northern Quebec who were relocated during the 1950s.

The most surprising element of the removal operations carried out during the twentieth century is probably their sheer extent. The few examples above speak to that. The reasons for these relocations, stated or not, give us considerable pause. The Royal Commission on Aboriginal Peoples endorsed numerous demands formulated over the last few decades by Aboriginals themselves. It recommended that exhaustive inquiries be conducted by an independent body, the Canadian Human Rights Commission, and that action be taken in the form of apologies, compensation and preventive measures to remedy the harm suffered by the displaced individuals and communities. By calling on Ottawa to recognize its responsibility for violating the fundamental rights of Aboriginal people by carrying out these relocations, the royal commission moved towards what Aboriginals have been requesting for many years. According to the commission, recognition of the harmful effects of these policies and of the government's responsibility is a prerequisite to beginning an indispensable process of healing.

In its declaration of reconciliation preceding the action plan that it made public in 1998 in response to the recommendations of the royal commission, the federal government noted that the disastrous consequences of government actions on the Aboriginal nations need to be acknowledged. It gave the relocation of Aboriginal people as an example of initiatives that caused fragmentation, disruption and, in some cases, destruction of these communities. The government did not, however, follow up on the recommendation to give the Canadian Human Rights Commission responsibility for holding inquiries into all complaints relating to population displacement. The various appeals and forms of pressure are likely to continue, especially in light of the Human Rights Commission investigator's finding that Ottawa's implementation of the relocation of the Inuit in the 1950s amounted to a failure in its fiduciary obligation towards Aboriginal people.

The fiduciary obligation forces the federal government to account, in court, for the discretionary authority that it exerts over Aboriginal people. Since 1984, when the courts first imposed this obligation, Ottawa has no longer been able to act with total impunity towards them. It must now take Aboriginal interests into consideration, not just its own. If it is proved that the government is not doing so, it can be forced to pay compensation to Aboriginals.

In the case of the Mushuau Innu of Labrador, the Human Rights Commission investigator found that the federal government failed to fulfill its fiduciary obligation by neglecting, over a period of almost fifty years, to provide them with services equivalent to those it provides to other Aboriginals in Canada. It can therefore be anticipated that Aboriginal people will appeal to the courts to gain compensation for the wrongs they suffered as a result of relocation operations.

[1] Canada, Parliament, House of Commons, *Debates*, 3rd Parliament, 3rd Session, March 30, 1876, p. 933.

[2] I deal with this question in my book *Le statut juridique des peuples autochtones au Canada*, p. 40ff.

[3] Quoted in P.A. Cumming and N.H. Mickenberg, eds., *Native Rights in Canada*, 2nd ed., p. 331.

CHAPTER 3

Aboriginal Resistance

Throughout the history of the American continent, Aboriginals have refused to be controlled by other people's rules. While their refusal has taken many different forms over the years, since the mid-twentieth century its primary focus has been a desire not to allow others to define their individual and collective lives down to the smallest detail. Aboriginals want to correct the caricature of them that has been handed down and introduce their own point of view. The wrongs that have been done to them by various regimes need to be recognized and compensated. Further, the historic treaties signed with Aboriginal peoples must be respected and those that have not been implemented in one way or another should be put into effect. Even contemporary arrangements such as the James Bay and Northern Quebec Agreement are sources of litigation. Legal recourse is increasingly being used to overcome a lack of political recognition. Aboriginal peoples want not only freedom from the guardianship they have lived under, but also recognition of their right to establish their own institutions. And finally, they want society to take responsibility for the disastrous consequences of the Indian and Inuit population displacements that took place all across Canada.

A new reading of history

Aboriginal people note that since their first contact with the Europeans who came to America, accounts of their relations with whites have maligned and caricatured them. Their own point of view seems never to have been taken into account and has been presented only in a marginal way. Historical documents, which have served as the basis for textbooks and other sources of historical information, described the

79

relationship only from the colonialists' point of view. Government and parliamentary archives reflect the attitudes of elected representatives in successive regimes and the prejudices underlying colonization. In applying and interpreting legislation, the courts have accepted the colonial perspective and denied Aboriginals' rights.

This whole tendency relates to the colonial concept that superior (European) races had the duty to civilize inferior ones — the "pagan" civilizations that occupied land coveted over the centuries by the European powers. Missionaries picked up this notion and adapted it to their own goals. Colonization was a means to evangelize indigenous peoples, bringing them out of their condition as idolators into eternal salvation. The "duty" to colonize America came from a belief in the superiority of European civilizations and a patronizing view of non-European ones. Steady progress resulting from advances in European scientific knowledge sustained this belief.

Colonization and evangelization, supposedly founded on noble intentions, would eventually have to be accepted by the people they targeted. Parliamentary and government archives, historical documents and court rulings contain much evidence of the persistence of this way of thinking even today. We have not yet taken the opportunity to reexamine the founding themes of what is now America, and particularly Canada. In a view that still prevails, Aboriginal people have been slow to realize the value of our scientific achievements and have unwisely shunned them.

Aboriginals attack this kind of belief when they accuse Canada of being a settler state. They refuse to accept the refrain that they must get on board the train of progress and forget their old recriminations about the poor treatment they received. They find simplistic the argument that since the events in question happened long ago and we were not around at the time, we are not responsible for the current situation, deplorable as it might be. In any event, it was our French or British ancestors who behaved that way (some say that the English were better than the French, while others say they were worse).

Aboriginals demand first of all that their point of view be heard. For them, the lack of historical documentation directly recounting the Aboriginal version of events should not prevent us from reexamining history and reestablishing the facts in a way that takes into account Aboriginal contributions to what has become twenty-first-century Canadian society. According to Aboriginal people, a retelling of history would allow us to correct the essentially derogatory image of them that has developed among the general public. Some believe that, in the absence of Aboriginal sources, the best thing to do is to reexamine existing historical documents to extract the Aboriginal view. They argue that the documents, although written by Europeans and there-fore incomplete, can be analyzed from a perspective that makes it pos-sible to draw a fairer picture of Aboriginal people.

Others argue that the historical sources are totally biased and there-fore cannot serve as a base for establishing a true portrait of Aboriginal people. Only Aboriginals can speak in their own name. To remedy the lack of primary Aboriginal sources, they suggest replacing current his-torical sources with an "autohistory" told by the contemporary descen-dants of the Aboriginals who were in America at the time of contact with the Europeans. As the Royal Commission on Aboriginal Peoples put it, "Until the story of life in Canada, as Aboriginal people know it, finds a place in all Canadians' knowledge of their past, the wounds from historical violence and neglect will continue to fester — denied by Canadians at large and, perversely, generating shame in Aboriginal people because they cannot shake off the sense of powerlessness that made them vulnerable in the first place."[1]

Those supporting an Aboriginal autohistory believe that Aboriginal people had a greater influence on the Europeans who came to America than the Europeans did on them. They argue that the American Aboriginal cultural entity is still alive. Furthermore, at this time of cri-sis in western societies, it is needed as a beacon to Euro-Americans who must abandon their anti-ecological values. They believe a "renaissance" of Aboriginal thought will become an important phenomenon across the American continent and its influence will grow as ecological aware-ness increases on a world scale. The Aboriginal concept of the "sacred circle of life," which recognizes the interdependence of all living beings and promotes egalitarian relations with other creatures, would favour abundance, equality and peace on earth. This view is in complete opposition to the hierarchical evolutionary approach, which sees species as unequal, with inferior species eventually replaced by others that are better adapted in evolutionary terms.

For supporters of an Aboriginal autohistory, the science of history must stop concentrating primarily on the study of documents and objects and look instead to Aboriginal people, who left relatively little in the way of written materials, and to their oral tradition. Since Aboriginal values are still alive, history can no longer ignore them. To do so is to perpetuate its prejudice against societies that do not have a written tradition. Only by seeking out the ideas and feelings of people who make up Aboriginal societies today can history contribute to righting the wrongs that it has caused through the centuries to those societies.

This idea of recasting history from the testimony of descendants of Aboriginal people raises major methodological problems. For example, what value would one attribute to contemporary testimony that contradicts historical documents? And how could the notion of Aboriginal societies as a kind of ideal model be reconciled with historical accounts of wars between various Aboriginal nations who were fighting for control of the American continent at the time the Europeans came on the scene?

Nevertheless, this current of thought among Aboriginals stands as a strong reaction to their marginalization and indicates their desire to have the full range of their contribution to Canada known more broadly. I have already said that I believe a retelling of history is necessary. It would not involve reinventing documented historical events but rather looking at those same events through another lens, in an effort to introduce the Aboriginal as well as the European perspective. This retelling would require a reinterpretation of history in light of changes in our understanding of human beings.

The historical conception of Aboriginal peoples favoured by

European societies stemmed from theories that were used to justify their colonial aims and interests. This world view also allowed colonizers to justify their attacks on the integrity of these societies, some of which were completely destroyed. It is therefore not surprising that the historical documents clearly give the advantage to the Europeans and neglect to highlight aspects that could have tarnished their favourable image. A retelling of history is all the more necessary since historical accounts frequently contributed to the marginalization of Aboriginal people by caricaturing them.

Recognizing and remedying past wrongs

Aboriginal people want this retelling of history to be accompanied by a recognition of wrongs that were done to them, and they believe that those who caused the wrongs should assume full responsibility. The special system reserved for them led to the breakdown of their cultures, which brought about the social disintegration that continues today. As we have seen, the legitimacy of Canadian governments is seriously tainted, particularly because they so long deprived Aboriginal people of the fundamental right to vote. After five years of work and public hearings carried out all across Canada, the Royal Commission on Aboriginal Peoples observed in 1996 that "strong arguments are made, and will continue to be made, by Aboriginal peoples to challenge the legitimacy of Canada's exercise of power over them."[2] In addition to the rights they have been denied, Aboriginal people's challenges to the Canadian government focus on the panoply of measures adopted over time, whose cumulative effect has been to bleed many communities dry.

In the case of Indians in particular, some measures were directed at communities, such as those aimed at marginalizing traditional Aboriginal political structures and preventing the practice of Aboriginal culture, under threat of legal action. Other measures involved forced "emancipation" of individuals. For example, an Indian woman who married a non-Indian was deprived of her Indian status, while this was not the case for her brother who married a non-Indian. In education, a foreign language was imposed on Aboriginal children — French or English, depending on the religious community running the school. In addition, children were taken away from their families at a very young age to residential schools, which, as has been revealed in recent years, were places of abuse and cruelty.

Indians criticize political and religious authorities for adopting a policy of assimilation that involved taking young children away from their communities, often against their parents' wishes, and keeping them by force in the residential schools, where their native language, culture and social practices were forbidden and any transgression was severely, even brutally, repressed. While they were at these schools, many children were victims of assault and physical and sexual abuse that caused irreparable harm. Many victims grew up in silence and shame, especially since the veil was only recently lifted from the cruelty that took place in residential schools from the late nineteenth century up to the 1980s. Even now, we are only beginning to document the conditions that prevailed in the residential schools. The communities from which these children came also suffered as the after-effects of such ill treatment prevented many from playing an active role in their communities as adults.

All of these measures left a profound mark on individuals and communities. Aboriginal people are less and less willing to accept these things as regrettable administrative errors of a bygone era. They refuse to let the residential schools question go until the responsible authorities acknowledge the wrongs committed. They will no longer be content with the extreme restraint with which political and religious authorities have approached the matter for the last half-century. The government's efforts to avoid the political and legal costs associated with addressing these issues fully will no longer do for them. They will no longer be satisfied with the kinds of settlements that authorities set out for them to suit their own interests. The flood of legal actions brought in the last few years by individuals and groups against the federal government and various religious communities who were responsible for Aboriginal education offers eloquent testimony to this.

The emotional outpouring began in the early 1990s when Phil Fontaine, then Grand Chief of the Assembly of Manitoba Chiefs (later Grand Chief of the Assembly of First Nations), announced that he himself had been a victim of abuse at a residential school when he was a child. Various reports assessing the residential school system had pointed out significant deficiencies, but had not addressed the issue of abuse. The entire system was later brought to light and those in charge held responsible for having created and run it in full knowledge of what was going on.

For Aboriginal people, Ottawa's establishment of a $350 million healing fund to help victims of residential schools is both unsatisfactory and insufficient. The fund was announced in 1998 as the government's response to recommendations made by the Royal Commission on Aboriginal Peoples, which had examined the tragedy in great detail. Along with the announcement came a statement of reconciliation by the federal government towards Aboriginal people. The government noted the importance of healing the wounds left by the past. Toward that end, it expressed "profound regret" for its actions, which had "contributed to these difficult pages in the history of our relationship together,"[3] including its role in the creation and continuation of residential schools.

The combination of a relatively small amount of money, considering the extent of the damages caused, and the careful wording that limited the government's statement to regrets instead of apologies, left the Aboriginal community upset and angry. Ottawa has continued to refuse to apologize to Aboriginals. It fears the legal consequences that might follow in the lawsuits already underway against it and the additional ones that would likely be launched. For their part, Aboriginal people note that Ottawa publicly apologized for its poor treatment of Japanese Canadians during the Second World War. They figure that it should do at least as much in their case, not only for wrongs caused in the residential schools but also for the disastrous consequences of the government's policy of assimilation in general.

The same day that it announced creation of the $350 million healing fund, the federal government also announced that it would pay $1 billion to cancel a contract to build helicopters. Cancellation of this contract had become a major campaign issue for the prime minister. The disparity between these two amounts seemed to reflect the different weights that the government accorded the two issues. It could only be perceived as a public relations failure and a lack of sensitivity towards Aboriginal Canadians, for whom implementation of treaties signed by governments counted just as much as reparations for harm caused by the residential school system.

Respect for past treaties

While they aimed to subjugate the indigenous peoples, the European nations were not in full control of the situation when they arrived in America. Since Aboriginal people represented an established political and military force, the British and French agreed to treaties with them to further their settlement enterprises. Sometimes they would ally with a group to secure its aid or to obtain its agreement to stay out of conflicts between the European nations. At other times they joined with one Aboriginal nation to support it in a fight with another Aboriginal nation. These alliances were frequently formalized through treaties that declared their peace and friendship. They differed from the later treaties of the nineteenth and twentieth centuries in that they involved no surrender of Aboriginal rights.

Surrender treaties became more common in Canada after the American War of Independence (1775–82), which led to a wave of Loyalist immigrants fleeing the United States and coming to Canada. Many of the Loyalists came to Ontario and settled in areas that Britain acquired through treaties with the Indians, who gave up ancestral title to their traditional lands. The Manitoulin treaty in 1836 and the Robinson-Huron and Robinson-Superior treaties in 1850 were signed in this way.

After Confederation in 1867, Canada continued Britain's imperial policy, as laid out especially in the Royal Proclamation of 1763. In line with this approach, it signed treaties in which Aboriginals surrendered territorial rights to their traditional lands. In return, the government established reserves for the signatory groups and paid them compensation, in the form of annual rent. The compensation was insignificant in relation to the immensity of the lands that were now free of Aboriginal title. Some treaties provided medical services, medical supplies or even farm equipment — this was a period when the government wished to have the Indians, who were still nomadic, settle into an agricultural way of life. Between 1867 and 1930, thirteen such treaties were signed with a variety of Aboriginal groups, from Ontario all the way to northern British Columbia and in parts of the North and Northwest. The federal government entered into these treaties before some of the western provinces existed as such.

Canadians have a tendency to minimize the current value of these treaties. They do not understand why they must still be tied to these historical documents, especially since the documents testify to a bygone era, in which Aboriginals' political and economic situation differed completely from the position they occupy today. There is also a general reluctance to recognize the legal value of historical documents involving Aboriginal peoples. This reluctance is all the more striking when compared with how little we question other historical documents, such as those recording the capitulation of Quebec in 1759 or the fall of Montreal in 1760, or the Treaty of Paris that followed in 1763, in which France ceded its American territories to Britain. In the wake of the Treaty of Paris, King George III of Britain signed the Royal Proclamation of 1763. Why would one part of that text, setting out the administration of the newly acquired territories, carry weight, while another part, recognizing the rights of "the several Nations or Tribes of Indians," would not?

Aboriginal people view these treaties as completely valid and feel they should be honoured. They nevertheless find the treaties quite problematic. First, many Aboriginals, while not questioning the legal consequences of signed treaties, have strongly criticized the process that produced them. They point out that the Aboriginal signatories were clearly disadvantaged by the fact that all negotiations took place in a language foreign to them. Furthermore, they had no way to verify that the final text truly represented the terms agreed on during negotiations, as the treaties were written in English. In addition, the concept of land ownership used by the Canadian legal system was completely unfamiliar to them. Finally, they trusted the word of government representatives, although in many cases the government did not carry out the promises it made in the treaties. For Aboriginals, it is important to return to the kind of formal relationship that treaties between nations represent. According to them, the recognition of treaty rights in Canada's 1982 constitution confirms the current legal validity of these historic commitments.

Aboriginal people consider it equally important to correct past omissions and start applying those terms of the treaties that have not been respected up to now. Government archives contain numerous examples of treaties that were not respected and Aboriginal complaints about this negligence. Their constant appeals finally led the government to adopt a policy in 1973 aimed at dealing with their grievances. The Specific Claims Policy, as it is called, is applicable to Indian complaints that their land was poorly managed or that treaties signed with them were not respected. Under the policy, the government will consider itself accountable for dealing with these cases only when it has been established that it failed in its "legal obligations" by not respecting a treaty or agreement signed with the Indians.

Indians strongly criticized this policy from its inception, in part because the government gave itself the role of both judge and party to the case. The government decides whether or not to approve the financing of a claim, judges its merits, defines the parameters of any negotiation regarding claims that it considers well founded and the terms of any settlement to be made, all while playing the role of the other party in the negotiation. Some modification has been made to the process with the establishment of an Indian Claims Commission that examines, analyzes and makes recommendations regarding claims rejected by the government. By and large, however, the policy remains intact and subject to the same criticisms. Increasingly, there is pressure to establish an independent and impartial tribunal to deal specifically with these legal claims.

Two examples, involving the Indians of Saskatchewan and the Huron-Wendats of Quebec, offer an idea of the extent of potential litigation. The Canadian government, the Saskatchewan government and some Indian bands living in the province concluded a tripartite agreement under the Specific Claims Policy in 1992. The agreement was designed to address Ottawa's failure to implement some of the clauses of treaties signed in 1874 (Treaty No. 4), 1876 (Treaty No. 6) and 1906 (Treaty No. 10). Under the treaties, one square mile of land for each Indian family of five, or 160 acres for each individual Indian, was to be assigned to the signatory bands. This was not carried out in full. The province of Saskatchewan, established by federal legislation in 1905 (after the first two treaties had been signed and before the third), is party to the accord because the federal government transferred ownership of land in the province to it in 1930. This transfer was conditional on the province's making available, on request, any land Ottawa needed to comply with the treaties it had signed with Saskatchewan's Indians. This land therefore falls under federal administration while being owned by the province. Thus, according to the agreement, the province should transfer these lands that had been promised to the Indians but never given.

As sufficient land to fulfill the promise was no longer available, the parties agreed that the bands would receive monetary compensation instead. The amount of compensation was based on a complex calculation that factored in the area of the land that the Indian bands should have received more than a century ago, equity and population growth in the twenty-four affected communities. In the agreement's preamble, Ottawa acknowledged that some of the obligations flowing from the treaties had not been fulfilled and that compensation of $427 million must now be paid. The Indians of Saskatchewan had thus been deprived for more than a century of lands that Ottawa had promised to transfer to them in return for having surrendered their ancestral rights — lands that represented a tiny fraction of the ancestral land ceded by the Aboriginals. These lands have been lost forever, even if the Indians were compensated a century later.

Under the same policy, Ottawa also paid compensation to the Huron-Wendat nation living in Quebec. This payment was related to the illegal relinquishment of a reserve of forty arpents (fourteen hectares) given to the Huron-Wendats by the Jesuits in 1742. These lands were ceded to the federal government in 1904, in return for compensation. The cession was considered illegal because the minister of Indian affairs did not meet all the legal requirements regarding a referendum that an Indian band must hold among its members before it can agree to surrender any part of reserve land. Several Quebec City suburbs were later developed on the ceded land, which rendered restitution to the Huron-Wendats impossible. For many years Ottawa systematically refused to take action. Finally, the government consented to negotiate the issues in dispute. On May 8, 2000, the parties reached an agreement involving a payment of $12 million. In this way, the bureaucrats' negligence led to government responsibility, which required payment of a second indemnity after so many years. It would have been preferable for the Huron-Wendats to keep the land, which they could have used to accommodate their population growth over the years. Because of this incident, the Huron-Wendats found themselves in a small enclave at Lorette — so small that the government was forced to buy back more land to add to it. Ottawa thus had to spend public money three separate times during this affair. It would have been less expensive to have allowed the Huron-Wendats to maintain ownership of the fourteen-hectare reserve.

Legal recourse in the absence of political recognition

Not all lawsuits between Aboriginal people and the federal government relate to old treaties. Questions regarding implementation of contemporary agreements also generate their share of conflicts. Since the

James Bay and Northern Quebec Agreement was signed in 1975, it has spawned multiple lawsuits by one of the signatories, the Cree Indians. The Crees explain their decision to resort to the courts by citing inadequacies and delays in implementing the agreement. Their complaint echoes that of Aboriginals across Canada, who note the government's abysmal record with regard to respecting the historic treaties it signed. For the Crees, as for Aboriginals in general, the courts have appeared to offer a forum in which to fight the lack of action on their political concerns, although for a variety of reasons Aboriginal people have not always used the court system. Before the 1960s, Aboriginal people brought relatively few lawsuits aimed at gaining recognition of their rights. Beginning in the sixties, Indians began to appeal to the courts for recognition of their rights after federal and provincial legislation presented increasingly serious impediments to their collective and individual activities.

From 1927 to 1951, federal law prohibited anyone from earning money by making claims on behalf of an Indian or an Indian band without first obtaining permission from the superintendent general of Indian affairs. Effectively, Indians could not pursue their legal rights without the consent of the federal government. Government authorities argued that the rule was justified to protect Indians from exploitation by lawyers and others. Under this system, the government had the power to refuse all challenges to the regime it had put in place. Several organizations representing Indians continued to pursue their rights to Canadian territory, despite the legislative and administrative measures that had been adopted to suppress these rights. These groups were considered agitators who had to be contained, and controlling Indian lawsuits was one way to achieve this goal. Not surprisingly, during this period, courts decided cases concerning Indians in their absence.

From the time of Confederation in 1867, Canadian courts have generally interpreted the law narrowly and only in very exceptional cases recognized Indian rights, even when historic treaties explicitly promoted them. Struggles over these issues commonly took the form of cases relating to traditional activities such as hunting and fishing, in which

Indians would invoke their rights as the original occupants of the land to fight the application of federal or provincial laws. Legal decisions gradually reduced Indian hunting rights as the courts judged that such rights could be limited by federal legislation.

We have already seen that a number of such decisions came from the judicial committee of the Privy Council in London, which acted as the court of last resort for Canada from 1867 to 1949. Thus, the major decisions that shaped judicial interpretation of the Canadian constitution were made by British judges during the first eighty years of Canada's independence. Notably, they were responsible for establishing the rules defining the division of legislative powers set out by the constitution. We must remember that questions of Indian rights were largely decided in their absence, in cases focused on the division of power between the federal and provincial governments. The *St. Catherine's Milling & Lumber Co.* decision rendered by the Privy Council in 1888 was the first relating to Indian rights in Canada. It recognized that Indians have limited territorial rights based on the Royal Proclamation of 1763. According to the Privy Council, Indians were entitled only to those rights that were expressly given, in the Proclamation or elsewhere. This decision laid the foundation for all subsequent ones regarding Aboriginal rights in Canada until the 1970s.

Two lawsuits brought by Indians in the early 1970s would have a profound influence on jurisprudence in this area: a challenge brought by the Cree Indians of Quebec to a provincial government hydroelectric project in northern Quebec, and a request for declaratory judgement by the Nisga'a Indians of British Columbia. These offer two examples of a legal strategy adopted by the Indians in the absence of a political will to recognize their rights. The strategy did not stem from trust in the courts, which had not shown themselves to be particularly open to recognizing Indian rights, but simply from a failure to achieve results on the political front. For example, by the late 1960s, Quebec Indians had stated their position concerning ancestral rights explicitly before both the Canadian and Quebec governments. However, the political negotiations begun at that time were never followed through, and were compromised by the announcement of the James Bay hydro-electric project in 1971.

The actions by the Crees and the Nisga'a were brought in an era when the federal government had publicly announced its intention to transfer its constitutional authority over Aboriginals to the provinces. The Cree case led to an out-of-court settlement that was formalized by the James Bay and Northern Quebec Agreement in 1975. The Nisga'a did not win in any forum to which they brought their arguments, and a Supreme Court of Canada decision ended the legal dispute in 1973. Although it was unfavourable towards Aboriginals, this decision created a line of demarcation in Canadian case law, causing significant political repercussions in the way land claims were handled.

As we saw in chapter 2, in the 1973 *Calder* decision the Supreme Court reversed the established jurisprudence that had followed from *St. Catherine's Milling & Lumber Co.* This reversal shocked the legal and political communities. The *Calder* decision came in response to a case brought by the Nisga'a, who argued that their claim to land in B.C. remained intact. The Indians lost the case on a technical point, and the court was divided on the question of whether such an entitlement could still exist in 1973 in a Canadian province. Three judges decided that the Nisga'a held a valid title, while three other judges ruled that the title had been extinguished by the actions of various governments. Most importantly, for the first time in Canada, the court based the existence of an Aboriginal title on the fact that the Aboriginal people were living in organized societies at the time of their contact with the Europeans and were occupying the land, as had their ancestors from time immemorial. The Aboriginals retained their title because of that occupation, regardless of whether successive governments had recognized rights flowing from it.

This decision caused an enormous shock, as it overturned the restrictive approach that courts had employed for almost a hundred years. From this point forward, Aboriginals would no longer have to demonstrate that specific rights had been expressly recognized. They would simply have to establish their connection with a group that occupied and used the land at issue at the time the Europeans arrived in America. Proof of occupation by a particular group has thus become the determining element in deciding Aboriginal title. The decision concluded the legal proceedings concerning the claims of the Nisga'a of British Columbia and brought the action back to the political scene.

Recognizing ancestral rights

The Supreme Court's decision in *Calder* caused the federal government to rethink its legal position. Prime Minister Trudeau had stated this position in 1969, when he said that the government would not recognize ancestral rights because it wanted to make Indians full-fledged citizens instead of a group apart as they had been in the past. Furthermore, while Ottawa recognized past treaties, they should have an expiry date, and future treaties appeared inconceivable. Admitting that the *Calder* ruling made this position untenable, the government adopted a new Comprehensive Land Claims Policy in 1973. Under this policy, it would negotiate Aboriginal land claims where a group's ancestral rights had not been extinguished by treaty or by some other means.[4]

Under the new policy, the lawsuits brought by the Crees of Quebec and the Nisga'a of B.C. had a political sequel. The James Bay and Northern Quebec Agreement, signed in 1975 by the federal and Quebec governments, was the first accord reached in this context.[5] Quebec Premier Robert Bourassa was motivated to find a solution that would ensure completion of the hydroelectric project and thus fulfill an election promise. By contrast, the agreement in the Nisga'a claim was not reached until 1998, a quarter-century after the Supreme Court decision and adoption of the new policy. The B.C. government refused for a long time even to consider the idea of participating in a tripartite negotiating process, which would eventually obligate it to grant additional land to the Indians in the province. Successive provincial governments maintained their opposition to the process for more than twenty years. The federal minister of Indian affairs finally convinced the province to participate after the "Oka Crisis" of 1990, which shook up the Canadian and Quebec governments. The minister suggested that since the land claims of the Mohawks of Kahnawake were an issue in the crisis, it should give pause to other provincial governments facing similar claims.

The agreement with the Nisga'a is the second comprehensive land claim agreement dealing with provincial lands. The James Bay (1975) and Nisga'a (1998) agreements are the only two tripartite agreements signed in the more than twenty-five years since the federal government brought in its land claims policy. In the meantime, Ottawa has resolved claims involving federal lands, where it has sole authority over the land in question, but other claims involving provincial lands remain unresolved.

Aboriginal groups lament the fact that, under the federal policy, their rights do not seem to carry enough weight to prevent the government from doing what it wants, so that the negotiation process becomes very slow. Their experience with tripartite land claim negotiations seems to prove the point. The James Bay and Northern Quebec Agreement was the only one completed within a relatively short period — three years. As we saw in that case, the Quebec government was motivated by election promises it had made.

On the other hand, negotiations on the Nisga'a claim dragged on for more than twenty-five years, from 1973 to 1998. Several dozen other land claims in British Columbia are still pending. Similarly, a land claim brought by the Montagnais and Attikameks of Quebec has been under negotiation since 1979, with no concrete results. Recent talks between the governments of Newfoundland and Quebec regarding a new phase of the Churchill hydroelectric development might have helped to accelerate negotiations with some of the Innu-Montagnais in Quebec. But a later decision to abandon this project removed any sense of urgency from the need to conclude an agreement about the land. And although the federal government acknowledged several years ago that a claim brought by the Algonquins of Quebec was well founded, no actual negotiations have started.

Aboriginal people have also severely criticized the government's expectation in its land claims policy that any agreement will be accompanied by the extinguishment of Aboriginal rights. Aboriginal parties must definitively surrender rights to their traditional lands, and these are extinguished, along with any other rights and appeals, when the final agreement is put into force. This condition stems from the government's desire to free crown title completely from any future claims of rights by Aboriginal parties. The government is prepared to pay for peace, but it wants to do so once and for all, making any reopening of the issues impossible. Once a final agreement is reached, the Aboriginal signatories can only exercise rights explicitly outlined in it. The Canadian government considers closing the door on future appeals an essential feature, which will ensure the finality that all parties to these cases seek.

This condition has always formed a crucial component of historic treaties and agreements. In this respect, Canada is continuing a policy that the British began in 1763. Aboriginal people have always opposed this precondition and have applied increasing pressure on Ottawa to eliminate it, but without success. It seems odious to them that the process for recognizing their specific, concrete rights is predicated on extinguishing their ancestral rights.

During negotiations on the Attikamek and Montagnais land claims, the Quebec government made it very clear that it did not agree with Ottawa's position on extinguishment of rights. In a 1978 meeting between Quebec Premier René Lévesque and several of his ministers on one side and Quebec's Indian chiefs on the other, the Attikameks and Montagnais asked the Quebec government to support them in dealing with Ottawa on this issue. The response was favourable: The Quebec government would no longer require extinguishment of rights as a precondition to signing an agreement. In practice, however, this support had little impact. The federal government maintained the requirement, and it had the last word on the matter through its exclusive power to adopt legislation extinguishing the surrendered rights in the wake of an agreement.

Aboriginal opposition to the extinguishment of rights on reaching a land claims agreement took on a new dimension after the constitutional changes of 1982. Several Aboriginal groups once again demanded that Ottawa withdraw this requirement. They argued that since the Canadian constitution now recognizes Aboriginal ancestral rights, extinguishment of those rights no longer has any basis. The rights now had special protection under the constitution, so that they were at least partly sheltered from legislation. Before 1982, Ottawa had justified the extinguishment of rights by arguing that they were not recognized by the constitution, and this argument could no longer hold.

Further, Aboriginals concluded that since 1982 the federal government no longer had the power to extinguish ancestral rights unilaterally, as the courts had given it permission to do before that date. This is exactly what Ottawa did in 1975 when, in reaching a deal with the Crees and Inuit, it eliminated rights held by the Attikameks, Algonquins and Montagnais in northern Quebec without their consent. This situation could not occur in the new constitutional regime. Recognition of ancestral rights in the Canadian constitution shelters those rights from unilateral extinguishment.

For Aboriginals, the extinguishment issue always raised a major stumbling block to signing land claims agreements. This issue was also behind 1982 appeals made by the Quebec Crees in which they argued that only some of their rights were terminated when they signed the James Bay and Northern Quebec Agreement. According to them, a wide range of ancestral rights remained, including the inherent right to self-government, as these rights were not explicitly surrendered in the 1975 agreement and have since become recognized and protected by the constitution.

The Royal Commission on Aboriginal Peoples supported this position. In its 1996 report, the commission stated that the current federal land claims policy should be replaced with a new process "that is less exclusionary with respect to the parties and the subject matter of agreements and predicated on the affirmation rather than the extinguishment of Aboriginal title."[6] In its response to the Commission's report, made public in 1998, the federal government indicated its readiness to explore other possible methods of agreement that could provide certainty, but it did not elaborate on this statement. The definitive nature of any resolution lies at the heart of this notion of certainty sought by the government. Only a final agreement, Ottawa maintains, can completely protect governments from future or ongoing land claims. This element is the main source of Aboriginal opposition to the policy.

The nature and status of Aboriginal title has begun to attract the attention of the courts. The Supreme Court has rendered ten or so decisions since 1990 in which, on the basis of the specifics of each case, it has delineated concepts relating to ancestral rights, rights flowing from treaties, existing rights and Aboriginal title, now protected by the constitution. The first definition of Aboriginal title offered after 1982 arose from the *Delgamuukw* decision. The Supreme Court held that Aboriginal title constitutes a type of ancestral right protected by the 1982 constitution. The court further specified that while Aboriginal title falls under the category of ancestral rights, it includes unique characteristics that distinguish it from other ancestral rights.

This means that, unlike an ancestral right to fish, for example, Aboriginal title now consists of a right to use the land that is not limited to traditional and habitual pursuits. Use of the land might take many forms, as is the case on Indian reserves where we see everything from public to private residential to industrial and commercial use. The Supreme Court further held that Aboriginal title also includes mineral rights, confirming the right to use the land for mining purposes, a use that is not traditional for Aboriginal people. The court relied on the fact that federal law already governs mining on reserves in concluding that Aboriginal title need not be restricted to traditional land use.

The Supreme Court did, however, place special limits on the scope of Aboriginal title. The court distinguished Aboriginal title from complete ownership, making it a unique type of land holding. This means that the usual rules relating to property rights cannot be applied. The land may not be used in a way that is incompatible with its current occupation or with the Aboriginal people's long-term connection to it, unless the Aboriginal people first cede title to the crown. Thus, Aboriginal people are prohibited from using land to which they hold Aboriginal title in ways that will compromise its value. To illustrate the point, the court noted that putting a parking lot on land that has significant cultural value for a community would be considered an incompatible use. In such a case, the community would have to surrender its title to the government before proceeding. This limitation is designed to engender caution on the part of Aboriginal communities when deciding how to use traditional lands to which they hold Aboriginal title, since surrendering title to the government would severely limit their rights with respect to the land.

As with other ancestral rights, Aboriginal title is not absolute. It can be limited, but any such limitations must be justified according to the criteria defined in the jurisprudence. A government must first establish that the legislative objective it is pursuing is "compelling and substantial." The court has given a number of examples of objectives that would be considered justification for passing legislation or taking action that infringes on Aboriginal title, such as conservation of wildlife and fisheries, environmental protection, development of natural resources (mining and forestry), hydroelectricity, economic development, pursuit of social and economic fairness, the building of infrastructure and accommodation of the workers needed to build it, and recognition of the historical fact that non-Aboriginals depend on natural resources and participate in the extraction of those resources.

A government would also have to establish that its legislation or project is compatible with its fiduciary obligation to Aboriginal people. To assess this, the courts must examine whether the government in question took measures to mitigate the infringement. The Supreme Court defined a range of such measures, from an obligation to consult (this being a minimum requirement) to an obligation to gain consent in certain situations, including the adoption or amendment of legislation regarding wildlife conservation. The requirement therefore runs from the right to be consulted in all cases to a right of veto in some cases. Most often, it implies a right to participate in decision-making about the lands and resources through political negotiations undertaken in good faith in which all parties are prepared to compromise. The developing jurisprudence has only served to strengthen Aboriginal opposition to the extinguishment of their ancestral rights. Why should Aboriginal people sign agreements that will eliminate their Aboriginal title, when this title can give them the right of veto on certain development activities on the land?

There is another area where Aboriginal opposition to the current system has been clearly expressed for more than three decades. During this period, they have consistently demanded an end to government guardianship.

Moving away from guardianship

Since Ottawa's announcement in 1969 of its intention to transfer authority over Indians to the provinces, Aboriginal and especially Indian resistance to the status quo has been growing. In effect, Indians are opposing the very nature of the relationship — ward to guardian — that they have had with the government. Increasingly since 1982, rejection of the government's supervisory role has been evolving into a call for Canada to recognize a third order of government, an Aboriginal level that would operate parallel to the federal and provincial levels.

In the constitutional conferences that took place between 1983 and 1987, Aboriginals tried without success to obtain an amendment specifying that the rights recognized in 1982 included the inherent or unconditional right to self-government. The federal and provincial governments refused to establish a third order of government, although Ottawa did appear ready to recognize a conditional right to self-government, which could only be put into effect after its content was defined in an agreement with each Aboriginal group that wished to exercise it.

Both the provinces and the Aboriginals rejected the federal proposition. And as the constitutional requirement to consult with Aboriginal peoples had been satisfied through the constitutional conferences held between 1983 and 1987, issues concerning them were subordinated to other constitutional issues for the next three years, until the Meech Lake Accord was rejected in 1990. The 1987 talks surrounding Meech Lake dashed the enormous hope created by constitutional recognition of Aboriginal rights and greatly amplified Aboriginal frustration. Meech Lake, put forward by Prime Minister Mulroney and Quebec Premier Bourassa, was supposed to "correct" the isolation of Quebec during the repatriation of the constitution in 1982 and obtain Quebec's "acceptance" of the new constitution. Because the constitution was repatriated without its consent, Quebec has always challenged its legitimacy even though it applies to Quebec.

In the face of this initiative, which sought constitutional recognition for Quebec's distinct status, Aboriginals expressed considerable resentment of the apparent lack of interest in granting similar attention to their concerns regarding self-government. In this context, Elijah Harper, an Indian member of the Manitoba Legislative Assembly, undertook his dramatic campaign to block ratification of Meech Lake in June 1990. The constitutional amending formula required the provincial legislatures to ratify the accord. Harper opposed bringing forward the motion to accept the accord and ultimately prevented the Manitoba assembly from doing so. His action became the symbol of Aboriginal political resistance and frustration. If the process did not recognize their rights, Aboriginals could at least block it.

Many people, especially in Quebec, blamed Harper alone for the failure of the Meech Lake Accord. They did not blame Newfoundland Premier Clyde Wells who, after accepting the accord and promising to bring it before his legislature, failed to do so and was thus as responsible as Harper for preventing its ratification. It is noteworthy that the Oka crisis took place in July 1990, immediately after the rejection of the Meech Lake Accord.

The failure of Meech Lake was followed by new constitutional talks, leading to another agreement, the Charlottetown Accord. During these talks, the Royal Commission on Aboriginal Peoples endorsed the

Aboriginal position on the right to self-government, and Aboriginal leaders managed to have their concerns about self-government added to the text. The commission advanced a variety of formulas for formal recognition of a constitutional right to self-government in a commentary published in 1992, and restated its arguments in a report that appeared in 1993 — after the Charlottetown Accord, the second effort to adopt a constitutional accord in just a few years, had been rejected. Seeing the constitutional reform process as bogged down, the commission concluded that it was not necessary to wait much longer for Aboriginal self-government. There are good reasons to believe, it argued, that the inherent right to self-government is implicit in the rights recognized in 1982 — exactly the position Aboriginals themselves had taken from 1982 on. The commission's support, however, has not led to any actual gains. Aboriginal frustration has not diminished as recognition of their ancestral rights has not enabled them to gain more control over their affairs.

In its response to the Royal Commission recommendations, the federal government noted that it had recognized the inherent right to self-government and had adopted a policy aimed at implementing a greater level of autonomy. In fact, Ottawa was continuing to apply a policy that it had established back in the 1980s. Partly to respond to Aboriginal pressures and partly to create another opening in the constitutional impasse, the government tried to modify its approach to the management of communities and reserves. This new administrative approach, known as the self-government policy, looked to delegate federal powers of regulation, management or provision of public services to local band councils, tribal councils or service agencies.

Until the late 1950s, Ottawa had either assumed direct responsibility for providing services to Aboriginals or delegated it to various authorities. On many reserves, front-line health-care services are still provided in clinics that fall under the authority of the federal minister of health. In some cases, religious authorities offered educational services on Indian reserves in federal schools. Provincial authorities could also deliver educational services by receiving Indian students in the provincial schools or provide social services on the reserves. As the federal government did not want to handle all the services for Aboriginal populations, it paid for some services to be offered by these other authorities. In this context, Aboriginal people received services that had been conceived, regulated and negotiated without their input by the government and the service providers. As designated beneficiaries of these services, Aboriginals could not comment on the quality, relevance or method of provision of the services. Everything had been agreed on in their absence.

Pressure exerted by Aboriginal communities to improve public services and incorporate their participation in decision-making led Ottawa to gradually decentralize the delivery of services. It accomplished this through a variety of means, all of which included an element of communities, "taking charge" of their own affairs. At the beginning, the government only delegated management of certain programs, such as social assistance. Aboriginal authorities quickly recognized and condemned the limitations of this approach, which had them administering programs developed and regulated by Ottawa. They represented the government by distributing social assistance cheques, without any authority to address the deficiencies that their constituencies found in the programs. They were caught uncomfortably between their constituencies, which demanded improved services, and Ottawa, which imposed its restrictive programs on them.

In response to widespread Aboriginal dissatisfaction in the late 1980s, the minister of Indian affairs adopted new mechanisms for delegating powers, giving Aboriginals greater latitude in managing the resources coming from Ottawa through transfer payments. A number of agreements concerning transfer payments followed, either with local community authorities or with regional agencies. In 1993, Ottawa cast this latest approach as an expression of its desire to move from being a service provider to being a funding agency, helping Aboriginal administrations respond to the needs of their communities. It acknowledged that "the relationship between one government and another has become more complex and at times more difficult for all involved."

Self-government agreements vary according to the needs, interests and management abilities of the targeted communities. They might cover governmental and administrative institutions, the rules defining membership in the community, regulatory authority, land and resource management, transfer payments or services such as education, social services, culture, environment and administration of justice. In some cases, the Indian Act has actually been replaced with specific federal legislation. Thus, the Cree-Naskapi (of Quebec) Act, adopted to follow up on promises Ottawa had made under the James Bay and Northern Quebec Agreement and the Northeastern Quebec Agreement, grants more extensive powers to the Cree and Naskapi bands. Another example, this one in British Columbia, is the Sechelt Indian Band Self-Government Act.

The bipartite agreement signed in December 1994 between the federal government and the Assembly of Manitoba Chiefs, which represented sixty Indian communities in Manitoba, stands as a major initiative under this policy. This agreement sets up a ten-year bipartite negotiation process to establish a new relationship between Ottawa and the Indians of Manitoba, which is supposed to be based on mutual respect and recognition of the inherent right to self-government. It will be realized through dismantling the Department of Indian and Northern Affairs and abrogating the Indian Act with regard to Manitoba Indians, recognizing their governments, transferring federal powers to Manitoba Indians and otherwise "restoring" the governing powers they need to respond to their population.

The objectives outlined in this agreement are reminiscent of those Ottawa espoused in its 1969 policy statement: Dismantle the Department of Indian and Northern Affairs and transfer federal authority. However, one essential element of the 1969 policy has now disappeared. Where Ottawa had proposed transferring its powers to the provinces, now it has agreed to transfer them directly to Indian governments. The language has also changed since 1969. The Manitoba agreement speaks of developing and recognizing First Nations governments and "restoring" their powers, including jurisdiction over matters currently handled by Ottawa. The agreement foresees an end to application of the Indian Act to the extent required to promote a new relationship based on mutual respect between the federal government and the First Nations governments of Manitoba. It also raises the possibility that the two parties may invite the province to participate in further discussions, particularly where they involve issues relating to its role, such as education and social services.

Thus the process allows for bipartite agreements between Ottawa and Aboriginal people concerning provincial fields of jurisdiction, and shows once again how some federal policies impinge on provincial jurisdiction. The Manitoba agreement demonstrates just how reluctant Indians are to subject themselves to provincial authority, even in areas of provincial jurisdiction. They do not want to submit to provincial authority in areas where they can be directly responsible, even if that responsibility takes the form of authority delegated by the federal government.

This policy has particular implications for the government of Quebec. Quebec seeks to exercise as many powers as possible, including powers involving Aboriginal people, notwithstanding federal jurisdiction over them. The Quebec government finds itself in a novel situation. Unlike the other provincial governments, it has created specific political — if not strictly legal — obligations for itself. Through a cabinet decision in 1983 and a motion adopted by the National Assembly in 1985, it has recognized special rights for the province's Aboriginal nations and their right to self-government within Quebec.[7]

The general population does not grasp the symbolic and political scope of these two documents. Most Quebecers are not even aware of their existence, much less their content. Of course, successive governments have made no effort to bring these documents to the public's attention. Since their adoption, the government has continued to reflect on these questions and has issued several policy statements. The Quebec government appears to have chosen to codify these principles in an accumulation of agreements on a variety of subjects, either bilateral ones with Aboriginal nations or trilateral ones involving the federal government as well.

One thing is certain: Adoption of these documents has captured the attention of Quebec Aboriginals, perhaps especially Indians, and has had an impact on their efforts to obtain recognition of their right to self-government. Aboriginal people maintain that negotiations with the province should confirm their right to autonomy, while Quebec has traditionally used agreements to assert its authority over them. Here is a potential source of misunderstanding, at least if media reports and public opinion polls can be believed. These show that people do not understand the scope of the agreements that have been made public from time to time, presented as they are in a style and in terms that make them sound quite exotic for someone not familiar with the context.

The most recent agreement signed by the Quebec government and the Kahnawake Mohawks, made public in October 1998, offers an excellent example. The text of the accord provides for possible negotiations to reach specific agreements on topics such as administration of justice, taxation, public security and economic development within the Mohawk community. This text is preceded by a declaration of understanding and mutual respect, which includes the following statement: "With a strong sense of their respective culture, language, custom, laws and traditions, Kahnawake and Québec agree to negotiate with mutual respect for their national identities and each other's history and territorial occupation." This statement recognizes the distinctive elements of the Mohawk nation living in Quebec, and the Mohawks are surely expecting that the negotiations flowing from the agreement will take place in an atmosphere that recognizes their own national identity. However, it is considerably less clear what the statement means from the Quebec government's point of view.

In fact, the Quebec government did nothing to clarify the statement's meaning or to explain its political and legal context. The government did not try to bring this aspect of the agreement to public attention. Consequently, people are not aware of it and do not have sufficient information to judge its nature and scope. Agreements made with Aboriginals are perceived as promises to them, which could degenerate into litigation if the parties disagree. The misunderstandings generated by the secretiveness that surrounds the negotiation and conclusion of the agreements does not contribute to a healthy atmosphere as far as public opinion is concerned. On the contrary, they frustrate people, who have the impression that they are paying for a system that grants unjustified "benefits" to Indians. Meanwhile, the Indians are also frustrated, finding it extremely difficult to achieve the implementation of principles that Quebec has recognized for almost twenty years.

As much as Quebec is seen as deviating from the usual pattern in many aspects of the discussion on Aboriginal questions, there are two points on which all governments in Canada, including Quebec, agree. First, they all concur that Canada's sovereignty as a state comprises the federal and provincial levels of government alone. This would preclude a third, Aboriginal, level of government. It follows that these two levels of government operate on the basis that any agreements they sign involve a delegation of responsibility for services (such as social services, health and police) or management of an activity (such as hunting and fishing for purposes of providing food) to a particular Aboriginal authority. Second, all governments invoke the principle of territorial integrity and provincial ownership of land (or federal ownership in the case of the territories — Yukon, the Northwest Territories and Nunavut).

This position lies at the heart of Aboriginal people's challenge to the Canadian system, especially since 1982. They argue that this framework runs counter to their inherent right to self-government on their own land, with their own institutions, parallel to federal and provincial institutions. Some Aboriginals demand complete sovereignty, separate from that of Canada, but a larger number demand recognition of their sovereignty within the Canadian system.

The Supreme Court has not accepted the Aboriginal point of view regarding sovereignty. In the *Delgamuukw* decision, the court repeated what it and other courts had always said about the limits of Aboriginal title, namely that it does not call into question crown sovereignty in Canada. This legal confirmation has not diminished Aboriginal efforts.

They believe that their future depends on recognition of the right to govern themselves. Aboriginal people appear determined to obtain profound changes to the system of guardianship, which they refuse to see continue.

[1] Canada. Royal Commission on Aboriginal Peoples. *Final Report*, Vol. 1: *Looking Forward, Looking Back*, p. 7.

[2] Ibid., p. xxv.

[3] Canada, Department of Indian and Northern Affairs, *Gathering Strength — Canada's Aboriginal Action Plan*, p. 5.

[4] Details of this policy are analyzed in my book *La question indienne au Canada*.

[5] The circumstances surrounding the signing of the James Bay and Northern Quebec Agreement and the related litigation, which continues even today, are analyzed in my book *Tribus, peuples et nations*.

[6] Royal Commission on Aboriginal Peoples, *Final Report*, Vol. 2., *Restructuring the Relationship*, Part One, p. 70.

[7] These two texts are reproduced in English in Quebec, Secrétariat aux Affaires autochtones, *Partnership, Development, Achievement — Aboriginal Affairs Québec Government Guidelines*. A detailed analysis of these two documents appears in chapter 9 of my book *Tribus, peuples et nations*.

CHAPTER 4

New Solutions

The one point of universal agreement on Aboriginal questions is that the current situation has created deep dissatisfaction. One side of this dissatisfaction comes from Aboriginal people, who have been demanding radical changes for several decades. There are many reasons for their dissatisfaction and their aims are sometimes contradictory. Some Aboriginal people want to free themselves more or less completely from government guardianship. Others would prefer that the federal government, despite everything, continue to be the ultimately responsible party, because that will protect them from criticism and possible legal action from other Aboriginals. Some Aboriginal nations demand the right to maintain their traditional structures even when these deny full participation to women or other groups. Groups representing Aboriginal women, on the other hand, generally demand that the end of government guardianship be accompanied by the establishment of Aboriginal political structures that respect democratic rights and gender equality. These groups say out loud what many members of their communities will not allow themselves to say: They will no longer accept being subjected to arbitrary and discriminatory rule. Inuit communities, forming a substantial majority in the areas where they live, accept the idea of forming "public" governments representing all the residents of these areas, Inuit and non-Inuit alike. By contrast, Indian communities typically propose that participation in Indian government be limited to members of the community according to criteria that they define themselves.

The other side of the dissatisfaction comes from Canadians in general, who no longer agree to what they see as being largely a system of special treatment favouring Aboriginal people. The tax-exempt status of Indian reserves is coming under increasing criticism everywhere in Canada. In addition, once people find out what is really at stake in the Aboriginal land claims that the federal government has agreed to negotiate, they express their disapproval. The sustained opposition to the 1998 agreement that the governments of Canada and British Columbia signed with the Nisga'a Indians is an illustration of this tendency.

Since the mid-1990s, rejection of special rights for Aboriginal people has become a hobby horse for the main opposition party in the federal House of Commons. This sentiment, held by a segment of the Canadian population and expressed more openly in the west than elsewhere in the country, has been adopted by the western-based Reform/Canadian Alliance as its own. The Alliance argues that Aboriginal people should be put on the same footing as other Canadians, and receive no more than the same services that other Canadians do. This position goes against commitments made to Aboriginal peoples and obligations created by the recognition of special Aboriginal rights in the Canadian constitution since 1982.

There appears to be no clear idea of what objectives should be sought, and this inability to identify a consensus for the future represents one of the major difficulties in the current situation. Improving the living conditions of Aboriginal people is one objective. There could be others: improving Canada's (and Quebec's) image abroad and in international bodies, eliminating the pronounced socioeconomic disparity between Aboriginal people and the Canadian population as a whole, integrating Aboriginal people into Canadian society, ending discrimination against them, or soothing the troubled conscience that Canadians have regarding their relations with Aboriginal people.

Trying to find solutions or detailed blueprints for change without first establishing a consensus on objectives is a dangerous exercise. Hence, the mandate of a permanent political forum would need to begin with this task. It would be illusory to think that it could be done quickly and easily, but sooner or later the task will need to be undertaken.

Nothing will be resolved if we continue to make up Aboriginal policy as we go along, as we have been doing for a long time. Everyone is getting frustrated, because this option is expensive and never leads to long-term solutions. Whatever the current problem is, more public money is spent and a few programs and people are moved around, until the next problem arises with the same group or another one. The limits of piecemeal management have been amply demonstrated. There is no end to Auditor General's reports pointing out deficiencies in the management of public funds directed to Aboriginal people and the lack of accountability of Aboriginal authorities.

Media allegations in the fall of 2000 that public funds intended for rehabilitation services for Indians in Fort Alexander, Manitoba, were used to pay for a cruise for seventy rehabilitation centre employees and an assistant deputy minister at Health Canada only added to an already tarnished record. The refusal of Indian authorities to account for their use of government subsidies makes it impossible for the federal health minister to audit the use of these funds — in itself an argument for thorough change to the present system. In this case, the system has led to the use of funds that should have been directed towards improving the health of Aboriginal people for legal proceedings to obtain documents that will make it possible to audit the accounts.

The current situation penalizes everybody. It undermines the confidence both of Aboriginal people, to whom public programs are addressed, and of Canadians in general, whose questions about whether their tax dollars are being properly used are growing more insistent. It is doing increasing damage to the credibility of the federal government. It affects every Aboriginal community because people tend to generalize from each new problem that emerges. More and more voices are being heard, both in Aboriginal communities and elsewhere, demanding that a system of transparency and accountability be established in those communities.

Canadian authorities are responsible for creating a framework for discussion that will make it possible to define objectives for the future. These objectives will lead to discussions on the best instruments to use and paths to take to get there. It seems clear, for example, that the objective of improving the living conditions of Aboriginal people would lead to one set of actions, while that of improving Canada's image in international bodies would lead to quite another. We need to stop getting sidetracked and get on to the real issues. What are our true intentions towards Aboriginal people? Does the constitutional recognition of the collective rights of Aboriginal peoples represent anything more than one of a number of political elements that made it possible to repatriate the Canadian constitution in 1982? Since that time, the repercussions of this recognition have been determined in some detail by the courts, while efforts to implement Aboriginal rights at the political level are at an impasse. Does this mean that governments, intentionally or by default, have left this whole area to the courts? Can communities be left hanging indefinitely, as they are at the moment? Can arbitrary and often discriminatory administration within these communities be allowed to continue? Shouldn't we be supporting groups of people in these communities who are aware of the scope of the required task and are demanding that local Aboriginal authorities be made responsible?

A change in strategy

If a radical change in strategy is needed at this point, it is partly because of the way Canadian policy evolved over the last quarter of the twentieth century. In the 1970s, the government turned away from the colonial policies that had held sway previously and flatly contradicted some of the cornerstones of those policies. Thus, we have seen that in the wake of the 1973 Supreme Court decision in the *Calder* case, Canada decided to recognize the validity of Aboriginal title to Canadian territory, even in the absence of official recognition by successive governments. This new policy broke with earlier ones in which Aboriginal peoples were regarded as having only such rights as were explicitly recognized in laws or treaties.

Even more fundamentally, the recognition of Aboriginal rights in the 1982 constitution demands a radical change in legislative strategy on the part of governments, and especially the federal government. Whether they were passed before 1982 or since, federal and provincial laws can no longer be applied in the same way to Aboriginal people.

The political choice that Canada made in 1982 establishes a number of precedents that represent a departure from previous policies. First, Canada chose to recognize and confirm new rights for Aboriginals, grouped under two headings: ancestral rights and treaty rights. It also chose to recognize the existence of Aboriginal peoples — the only recognition of this kind in the Canadian constitution. Finally, by providing for a series of constitutional conferences on Aboriginal questions, Canada chose to involve Aboriginals formally in the constitutional process, as it never had before.

Thus, since the 1970s, Canadian policy has taken a sharp turn away from previous policies in certain areas, although it is still based on some of their major elements. For example, recognition of Aboriginals' ancestral rights can be seen as conflicting with the guardianship system under which Indians are governed. The federal government has also maintained since 1995 that it recognizes the inherent right of Aboriginal people to self-government. Before they can exercise that right, however, they will need to sign an agreement with Ottawa that will limit its scope. In other words, elements of government policy towards Aboriginal people are incoherent, or even flagrantly contradictory. As a result, these policies need to be thoroughly revised, and the various arms of the government that manage programs directed at Aboriginals need to be better coordinated.

A change in strategy towards Aboriginal people requires people to act and think in new ways. These new actions and reflections are primarily the responsibility of governments, but not exclusively so, as we will see in the following pages as we examine some of the required changes: amendments to legislation, reappraisal of recourse to the courts, the creation of a political and constitutional forum, the involvement of postsecondary educational and research institutions, the establishment of political and administrative institutions run by responsible authorities in Aboriginal communities, and negotiation with Aboriginal people in a new perspective. Finally, the development of international concerns in this area is a factor that can no longer be ignored. All the elements of this new strategy can be carried out simultaneously, and they will all require major commitments from the authorities responsible for them.

Changing the law

While it does not have priority over other elements, changing the law is essential in establishing a new strategy. The new legislation that ultimately emerges from this process will have an effect on the other elements. It will create a new frame of reference for the courts and influence the course of future negotiations with Aboriginal peoples.

Amendments to legislation must take account of the special constitutional rights for Aboriginal peoples recognized in 1982. In response to requests to determine the extent to which these new rights are protected from legislative infringement, the courts and especially the Supreme Court of Canada established criteria that federal and provincial legislation must henceforth meet to be applicable to Aboriginal people. Thus, if a federal or provincial law violates an ancestral or treaty right, it applies to Aboriginals only if this violation can be justified by appealing to more important principles. For example, if a government can demonstrate the need to preserve a particular species of game, then that would be an overriding principle that would allow it to restrict the exercise of Aboriginal hunting rights through legislation.

Aboriginals cannot exercise the rights that have been recognized since 1982 in total disregard for the law. The exercise of their rights must not compromise the preservation of species. But governments can no longer impose legislation on Aboriginal peoples without taking their special rights into account. As a result, existing laws need to be amended to adapt them to this new deal. Not every act will necessarily have to be amended, but every act will need to be examined to determine whether, *a priori*, it respects the criterion for justification developed by the courts. As the constitutional authority responsible for

Aboriginal people, the federal Parliament has adopted a number of general and particular laws applying to them. Some of these laws clearly need to be reviewed. The general law that governs Indians, the Indian Act, is an obvious example. Other general laws, such as the Fisheries Act and the Canadian Human Rights Act, will also need to be adjusted. Similarly, provincial laws, such as those dealing with wildlife conservation and natural resource development, will need to be submitted to close examination to bring them into compliance with the constitutional rights that have been recognized since 1982.

The whole Indian Act regime is based on Ottawa's discretionary authority over Indians and their lands, which does not respect the obligations imposed on governments since 1982. The government can no longer make decisions in Indians' name without at least consulting them. Hence this legislative and administrative regime needs to be reviewed in its entirety. In another area, the courts have stated that regulations under the Fisheries Act that affect Aboriginal people need to be changed. The minister of fisheries can no longer exercise discretionary authority in granting fishing permits to Aboriginals. The minister needs to adopt criteria that the department's civil servants will apply in deciding whether to grant permits. This is only one of the aspects of the Fisheries Act that needs to be reviewed. The Canadian Human Rights Act also needs to be reviewed, since depriving Indians of recourse to the act in discrimination cases contravenes their fundamental rights and goes against the federal government's fiduciary responsibility. These examples are a good indication of the scope of the revision that will be necessary.

In this new context, the courts have clearly said that constitutional recognition of Aboriginals' rights has given them a powerful negotiating tool when it comes to exercising these rights. Contrary to what many people believe, the courts are not wholly responsible for this situation. It follows logically from the political choice that was made in 1982 to protect Aboriginal rights in the constitution. For a number of years, there has been a widespread impression that the courts give everything to Aboriginal people. In fact, however, Canadians need to accept the consequences that flow from the choices made in 1982. Aboriginal rights need to be made concrete in the reality of the twenty-first century.

Nor should people think that they can escape this responsibility by trying to restrict these rights to activities and methods that prevailed in the seventeenth or eighteenth century. In the view of some, a hunting right guaranteed by a historic treaty could be exercised today only with methods that were in use at the time the treaty was signed. This is not the path that has been chosen in Canada, and the courts have made it clear that Aboriginal rights should not be interpreted in a manner that would fix them in time. It is an illusion to think that rights that Canada has chosen to protect could be capped in this way.

There are a number of ways of specifying the implications of these rights and thus establishing their limits. These different methods are not mutually exclusive and could be adopted parallel to one another. Canada could amend its legislation. It could negotiate in an attempt to define Aboriginal rights in general and particular agreements. The task of interpreting Aboriginal rights could be left to the courts. The primary strategy that has been followed since the late 1980s has favoured this last option. Aboriginal people have retreated to the margins of serious political discussion since that time.

Amendments to legislation are needed, but they also need to be accompanied by an assessment of the coherence of the programs and activities carried out under the authority of various federal departments. The effectiveness and cohesion of federal action with respect to Aboriginal people need to be examined in depth.

Rethinking the judicial route

As much as legislation needs to be changed, recourse to the courts needs to be reexamined. Recourse to the courts appears to be the only current method for defining Aboriginal rights, especially ones that have been recognized since 1982. Instead of the courts, political and social actors should be formulating public policy; the courts are playing a role that belongs in the sphere of public negotiation.

Of course, for governments, the main advantage of referring these matters to the courts is that it allows politicians to avoid responsibility for whatever is decided. Being free of this burden makes it easier to face the electorate when a decision is favourable to Aboriginal people, or to face Aboriginals themselves when it is unfavourable to them. On the other hand, the major disadvantage of allowing the judiciary to define the contours of Aboriginal rights is that this process is a long and costly one. The inevitable result of resorting to the adversarial court system is that a winner and a loser are declared, which does not argue well for relations between parties who will need to interact with each other.

Furthermore, when this route is followed, the necessary work of amending legislation is carried out piece by piece, often with only a single article of one law being dealt with at a time. Thus, if a case involves defining whether a given article of such and such an act can restrict the right of an Aboriginal group to fish for a specific species in a specific region using a specific method, the court has to limit its analysis to the particular case submitted to it. Since there are more than 600 Inuit and Indian communities in a position to claim rights of this kind, Canada's courts would be flooded with such cases if every possible variation of the questions currently on the table were submitted to them. The impression that the Supreme Court has been issuing Aboriginal rights decisions almost without interruption for more than a decade is not without foundation. This situation will continue as long as preference is given to the judicial option over the political one — legislation and negotiation. To be sure, the judicial option should not be eliminated. Nor is it realistic to think that it will not continue to be a favoured strategy both for governments and for Aboriginal people. But it should be used as a backup strategy, and not — as is currently the case — as the only way that recognized Aboriginal rights can be confirmed.

The Supreme Court's interpretation of recognized Aboriginal rights, developed since 1990, refers constantly to the need to negotiate with Aboriginals and to provide for their participation in decisions that concern them as well as in more general decisions that could modify their rights. The court has repeatedly reminded Canadians that negotiations are not only inevitable but also required. This in itself suggests that the judicial option as a primary strategy for defining Aboriginal rights is not an appropriate solution. The way it is currently used constitutes a waste of resources that should be devoted instead to improving the living conditions of Aboriginal people and working out new development strategies through negotiations with them. There are numerous drawbacks to the judicial option, two of which I would regard as especially significant. First, judges are not required to be accountable to Canadians for their decisions and the political and social effects of those decisions. Second, court decisions increase tensions between Aboriginal people and other Canadians, who have no part in the process and therefore see the situation as out of their control. In addition, the judicial option takes away the responsibility that citizens have for the commitments that politicians made in their name in 1982. Sooner or later, citizens will have to participate in the enormous task of defining Aboriginal rights, which should not be left to the bureaucracy or the judiciary.

Establishing a political and constitutional forum

Great expectations were created among Aboriginal people when they began to participate in the constitutional process dealing with questions that concerned them in the 1980s. Since the defeat of the Charlottetown Accord in 1992, nothing has been done to meet those expectations. A number of Aboriginal representatives have criticized Canadian political leaders, federal and provincial, for leaving them exposed in front of their constituencies. They had spoken to those constituencies in defense of the constitutional process, presenting it as a worthwhile initiative that could concretize their rights, and they had participated in the process in good faith. On the other hand, all the participants, representing governments and Aboriginals alike, knew that the constitutional process was a complex exercise in redefining the Canadian federal system, which would likely not produce quick results.

What has been most damaging since 1992 has not necessarily been the absence of short-term results, but rather the weakening of the credibility of Aboriginal leaders through the interruption of the process and the renewed marginalization of Aboriginal people. Once again, the good faith of governments has been called into question. Many Aboriginal people have found it increasingly difficult to avoid asking how Canada can recognize Aboriginal rights without specifying the way in which these rights can be implemented.

In this context, it seems to me that a permanent forum is an essential instrument. The establishment of such a forum would allow all the interlocutors — the federal and provincial governments and the various Aboriginal peoples — to create an overall political framework for discussions on a national scale. It would also allow Aboriginals to participate directly in these discussions. We need to find an instrument for bringing the definition of recognized Aboriginal rights into the political sphere. Such an instrument could at least help avoid loss of face by Aboriginal leaders, which could lead to the rise of people who are attracted to extreme positions. It could also bring Aboriginal questions back into the mainstream of public concern. This new attention to Aboriginal questions would be reflected throughout the political and administrative systems, and it would help enhance the credibility of those systems.

We should not expect that political and constitutional activity at the first ministers' level will in itself resolve all the outstanding points regarding Aboriginal people. The first ministers can give the impetus that is needed for change on this scale to take place, but the task is clearly too broad in scope to be completed through their work alone. Rather, it is a collective responsibility that needs to be exercised at all levels and by a variety of actors. This is why the permanent forum would need to be complemented by mechanisms on a regional or local scale that would be aimed at creating institutional links between Aboriginal people and political and administrative bodies at the provincial, regional, supramunicipal and municipal levels. Questions arising from the national discussions or ones that did not have national implications could be dealt with through these mechanisms. The idea that action at a grassroots level will occur in the wake of occasional meetings between first ministers and nationally elected Aboriginal leaders is an illusion. The current dynamic in which Aboriginals are engaged in keeping watch on Ottawa as it tries to download its authority onto the provinces, especially in the case of Quebec, also needs to be brought to an end.

Mechanisms need to be established at the intermediate and local levels so that ties can be established between communities (and their representatives) that currently live in ignorance of each other. This does not mean links between political institutions alone. Links between administrative institutions that provide public services — municipal bodies, county-level regional municipalities, hospitals, resource-extraction agencies — are also important. Bridges between institutions in Aboriginal communities and their counterparts in the surrounding communities are needed to end Aboriginal marginalization. The relations underlying these institutional links should be based on respect for all participants. It is essentially up to individuals to take initiatives in this direction, but they need to have institutional support and be part of a new vision of public-sector management.

Especially in isolated areas, neighbouring Aboriginal and non-Aboriginal communities function in parallel, sealed off from each other, to an extent that is difficult for people who have not been in that situation to imagine. The resulting waste of energy and resources, and therefore of public funds, should be enough to convince us of the need for change.

Thus, in the area of education, links could be established between school boards or some of the schools under their jurisdiction on one hand and band-run primary and secondary schools on neighbouring Indian reserves on the other. These links could take the form of student exchange programs, teacher exchanges or professional development for teachers, especially in isolated regions. Postsecondary training is another area where partnership links could be established.

In the area of health and social services, relations need to be established between hospitals and local health centres in Aboriginal communities. In this way, Aboriginals can receive basic care in their own communities while being provided with health services at a comparable level to other Canadians. In the current system, the federal government pays medical specialists who periodically offer services in Aboriginal communities. I am not suggesting replacing it with a system of direct purchase of health services by Indian bands from provincial hospitals. Rather, institutional links should be created between Aboriginal communities and provincial health networks. Such links would strengthen the local health infrastructure in Aboriginal communities and could lead to training programs that would allow Aboriginal people to take more responsibility for health care, at least in the area of basic services.

In the area of land development and land-use planning, formal links could be established so that county-level regional municipalities and local Aboriginal communities could share ideas, resources and services.

At least in the medium term, such institutional links should have a number of beneficial effects: better understanding between Aboriginal and non-Aboriginal communities, enhanced integration of Aboriginal communities into Canadian society and rationalization of public expenditures.

The responsibility of institutions of higher education and research

The change in strategy will need to go beyond the strict limits of the political and administrative spheres. Other social actors will need to contribute to the process as well, especially institutions of higher education and research. These institutions have a share of the collective responsibility in this regard, and it is essential that they fulfill this responsibility. In general, they have a social responsibility, and they receive public funds so that they can carry out their mission of training, education and reflection. The students to whom they must provide appropriate training are also citizens who are called on to contribute to their society and express themselves on social issues. At the same time, it is the duty of institutions of higher education and research to help society understand the internal and external factors that influence the course of its development. This reflective process should be directed towards an understanding of historical factors as well as current and emerging ones.

In how many universities are courses dealing with Aboriginals integrated into the programs of all faculties? If these institutions don't pay special attention to this aspect of Canadian society by incorporating it into their educational programs and by initiating research on Aboriginal questions, how can we say that they are satisfactorily fulfilling their central mission? When, in addition to these deficiencies, there are no programs for supporting or integrating Aboriginal students, how can universities provide those students with an adequate education? Canada could take its inspiration from initiatives established by other countries, such as Norway, which have created programs of this kind in some universities. Management faculties could offer programs tailored to the reality of Aboriginal communities to political and administrative actors in those communities.

With the myriad of new possibilities for adapting educational formulas available through distance learning and Internet communication, institutions could develop and set up programs for Aboriginals either on their own or in partnership with Aboriginal groups. Because Ottawa decided a few years ago to encourage increased autonomy and greater accountability for Aboriginal political and administrative authorities, the establishment of properly tailored programs for training Aboriginal leaders and public administrators has become an urgent priority. These should not be bargain-basement training programs with lower standards that would lead to discounted diplomas. Rather, they should consist of proper formal training with meaningful diplomas at the end. At the same time, they should be tailored to the realities in which Aboriginals live, taking account of such factors as distance from large urban centres, the need to master a second language and recognition of equivalent learning where appropriate.

Culture, history, health sciences, natural sciences, social sciences, education, psychology — in none of these areas have Aboriginal questions received sufficient attention in higher education and research in Canada. The initiatives that have taken place have generally been the work of individuals who have become interested in these questions, often in the face of the indifference or even resistance of their colleagues. Institutional responsibility is very different from these isolated initiatives. The current contribution of institutions of higher education and research to an understanding of Aboriginal questions leaves something to be desired in several areas. First, we don't have theoretical and practical studies of the impact of the socioeconomic system that governs Aboriginals on various aspects of their lives: acculturation, health conditions, short- and long-term psychological effects on individuals and communities, economic repercussions and so forth. In addition, we don't have comparative studies of these variables relating the situation of Aboriginals in Canada to that of indigenous people in other countries.

Nor do we have detailed studies of the way in which Canadian society has dealt with Aboriginal people. There are reasons why political scientists have said so little on these questions — as have jurists, historians and intellectuals in general. How can a society spare itself the task of doing research on the demands that Aboriginals have been expressing for the last half-century? How can it not try to determine the causes of those demands, especially in terms of the historical relationship between Aboriginals and other Canadians? How can it not seek to establish patterns of correspondence with similar demands elsewhere in the world? How can a society feel prepared to face its future when part of its population — a tiny part, to be sure, but a real one nonetheless — lives in conditions that are clearly inferior to those of its other citizens? And how can that society not worry about how perpetuating such a disparity will affect it in the long term?

Can we even talk about research carried out with and for Aboriginals, or with Aboriginals for the population in general? And what about research directed by Aboriginals? A partnership between higher education or research institutions and Aboriginals could help

enrich our knowledge in a number of ways. First of all, such a partnership would make Aboriginals direct participants in their education or
in research that concerns them, instead of objects of teaching or
research. In addition, it would make it possible for Aboriginals to be
involved in the development of courses or research guidelines, so that
they could make sure that education and research programs took
account of and were adapted to their points of view and priorities. It is
hard to see how university programs in public administration, political
science, law or history can be useful to Aboriginal people if they are not
tailored to Aboriginals who would like to work in their own communities. It is also difficult to understand why students in Canadian universities, some of whom will hold key posts in the public and private sectors and will be called on to establish relations with Aboriginal people,
are not made aware of these realities during their education.

The point is not to draw up an inventory of who is responsible for
what but to take stock of our collective ignorance in this area. This
ignorance has consequences for our capacity to identify solutions, as we
are constantly realizing that no information beyond the level of empir-
ical data is available. It is foolhardy not to correct this situation. It is in
the interests of society to know the different elements that constitute it
and to reflect on the challenges that confront it. No good can come of
putting off the moment when we begin this task, in light of the repercussions of the further deterioration that is likely to take place. Nothing
is forcing us to drift from crisis to crisis, without seeing these crises
coming and without analyzing them in between times.

In July 2000, the Montreal daily *La Presse* marked the tenth anniver-
sary of the Oka crisis with a series of articles, ending with a summary
analysis of the crisis. Two statements stood in contradiction to each
other: One person was quoted as saying that there was little chance that
something like the Oka crisis would happen again, while a spokesperson for Quebec's Indians said that very little had changed in the inter-
vening decade. What is most astonishing is that no substantial analysis
of the crisis, which shook numerous Quebec and Canadian institutions, has been carried out and made public. The Aboriginal leader's

statement should make us think because he predicted that difficult moments along the same lines could come again if nothing changes. His remarks indicate that Indians' dissatisfaction has not diminished since the crisis; it has remained stable at best and may even have increased.

The development of Aboriginal communities and individuals is at stake, as well as the development of Canadian society as a whole. We need greater control of the factors that affect this development. Each crisis makes us take another step in acknowledging our collective ignorance of the players and forces involved, leaving us with the disagreeable impression that we are not really on top of the situation. It is time for this state of affairs to change.

Suitable political institutions and responsible leaders

In light of the failure of the current guardianship system, establishing real Aboriginal governments with their own legal foundation appears to be a promising approach. The other elements of the new strategy will be truly meaningful only if they are directed towards this objective.

Achieving this goal will require a special effort on the part of Aboriginal peoples, who will need to contribute actively to defining structures that correspond to their values. Through reflection, they will need to identify the key elements of their cultures and define the rules under which they would like to be governed. These new structures should be given the responsibility of developing and ensuring broad public knowledge of laws and regulations. The laws should contain guarantees of equality and measures directed against discrimination caused by Aboriginal governments or individuals. There should be suitable judicial institutions responsible for applying these laws and obtaining redress when governments fail to respect individuals' fundamental rights. Legislation providing for transparency and accountability measures will also be needed so that Aboriginal governments will be responsible to their constituencies.

The system of tax exemptions for Indian reserves needs to be reviewed. At the same time, stable sources of financing need to be established to ensure the viability of Aboriginal governments. It is not realistic to think that ending the tax exemption will provide an adequate source of revenue for most of these governments under present circumstances. Income indicators show clearly that both individuals and communities have an extremely high level of dependence on governments. In light of this high level of dependence and the small size of many reserves, different methods need to be found to provide revenues for these communities. The imposition of royalties on the development and public and private extraction of resources in the areas where the communities are located would be one such method.

It is crucial to determine objectives in this area. If the aim is to make it possible for Aboriginal communities to improve their lot, then methods of financing that are radically different from the current ones need to be envisaged. When public subsidy formulas are readjusted over time, all that really happens is that the subsidies are given a new name and distributed in a different way. The basic fact that transfer payments of public funds are made does not change.

A goal of reducing the economic dependence of Aboriginal communities requires seeing their financing in a completely different perspective. It will not be easy for this new perspective to take shape. We will have to get rid of the image of Aboriginal people as dependents that has stuck to them for so long. Then we can look at applying financing formulas for their governments that we have never before thought of using. An equalization formula like the one that exists among provinces could be appropriate for Aboriginal governments as well. On the other hand, if we decide on more limited objectives, then it might be enough to look for new ways to cap increases in government subsidies. We would be aiming simply to contain the growth of public expenditures, which are currently at about $6 billion. Hence the time has come to ask fundamental questions about our overall orientation towards the future of Aboriginal people. The emphasis must now be placed on establishing this overall orientation, and then the necessary political, social, economic and other instruments would follow from it.

Finally, once objectives have been clearly defined, we will need to work out a timetable for the process of emancipation of Aboriginal communities. This is important not only for Aboriginals but also for society as a whole. The inevitable repercussions of the deterioration of living conditions and social disarray of Aboriginal people make emancipation a necessary goal. It would help them take responsibility for their current and future situation and bring to an end a system whose deficiencies have been abundantly demonstrated. What interest does the federal government have in committing itself ever more deeply to an expensive system that produces results that are either harmful or else so limited in their beneficial effects that they do not influence the overall course of events?

A timetable for emancipation would need to contain short-, medium- and long-term benchmarks that are sufficiently precise so that Aboriginal communities and the general population could keep abreast of the major steps in the process. The timetable would need to be negotiated with Aboriginal peoples and be directed towards the establishment of genuinely autonomous Aboriginal governments. To undertake a sociopolitical project of this scope, it will be necessary to agree on the terms and content of the changes that will take place. It will be just as important to establish realistic deadlines to give momentum to this ambitious project while taking its inherent difficulties into account. Simply encouraging Aboriginal communities to take full responsibility for their affairs is not enough. The benefits they will derive from this new status of responsibility over their current dependent status will need to be clear. Hence it will be important to have a clear idea of the objectives being sought — in contrast to the current situation, which creates the impression that confusion or even contradiction is the rule.

Negotiations in a new perspective

The new constitutional context that has prevailed since 1982 and the federal government's responsibility for meeting the obligations that the courts have imposed on it since 1984 also demand a change in perspective in negotiations with Aboriginal people. Consultation and negotiation with Aboriginals must be part of the process of examining all aspects of Aboriginal questions. The old perspective in which such negotiations were conducted — buying peace — is no longer appropriate. It is no longer possible to negotiate with Aboriginals in the spirit that has prevailed until now. In other words, governments can no longer choose at will whether to negotiate with Aboriginals, and they can no longer see Aboriginals as being in such a weak position that they will sooner or later need to accept the terms that governments define.

Aboriginals now have a clear legal basis for resorting to the courts if governments try to impose constraints on them without having at least consulted them. The Supreme Court has emphasized the importance of negotiations with Aboriginal peoples and the need for good faith and willingness to compromise on both sides. The court has also indicated that it will not hesitate to intervene to strengthen the negotiation process.

However, in the absence of any clear direction, improvisation has played a large role over the last three decades and continues today. No overall political objectives have been defined, so that it has been left to civil servants to act on their own. Many initiatives have been taken at the bureaucratic level, which have often overlapped with or even contradicted other initiatives. The impression has emerged that no one really knows what objectives should be pursued, but since the situation appears increasingly untenable all sorts of measures to improve it need to be tried. The ensuing confusion has become counterproductive, and political reflection has become imperative.

To bring about such a change in perspective in negotiations with Aboriginal peoples, the objectives being pursued need to be clarified. The way to do this is to identify the interests of the parties to the negotiations: the federal government, provincial governments and Aboriginal peoples. Once the interests of each of these parties and interests that they have in common are determined, the real issues in the required negotiations can be pinpointed.

There is another dimension to determining the interests of the parties. It is important that the issues be identified publicly and that Canadians in general get an idea of what is at stake before new legislation is adopted or an agreement with Aboriginal people is concluded. A process of identifying common interests and separating out competing ones will encourage Aboriginals to keep their expectations within bounds and allow governments to know how much room for manoeuvre they really have. There will be scope for public opinion to influence the process, in contrast to the present situation where government dealings most often take place behind the scenes and people are not in a position to assess what is at stake. In the current context, the only thing people in general can do is demonstrate their opposition to an agreement when they find out about it — in other words, when it has already been reached. British Columbians' acrimonious reaction after the Nisga'a land claims agreement was concluded illustrates this point.

Clarifying objectives and determining the interests of the parties will also make it possible to define more realistic parameters for negotiation. The parties will need to make an effort to have more specific objectives and to make these objectives better known.

Converging and diverging interests

The constitutional conferences held during the 1980s involved a large number of players, and this experience showed that in such a process interests combine in a variety of ways. Thus, the federal government does not always have the same interests as provincial governments. Some provincial governments may have common interests with the federal government but not necessarily with other provinces. In this sense, a single Canadian position, advanced by all the various governments, does not exist. On the Aboriginal side, each of the recognized Aboriginal peoples — Indians, Inuit and Métis — is represented by a number of political groupings. The three categories of Aboriginal peoples do not necessarily have common interests beyond the rather vague objectives of advancing the recognition of their rights. They can even represent opposing interests or express opposite positions. The Inuit, for example, favour public governments in which non-Aboriginals can be represented, while most Indians are opposed to such governments. Furthermore, different groupings within each of the Aboriginal peoples can have opposing interests. Thus, the interests of Indians whose ancestral rights were extinguished by treaties can clash with those of Indians whose ancestral rights have not been extinguished.

In a similar way but on a smaller scale, land claims negotiations under the policy established by Ottawa involve a number of players and a panoply of interests. When a claim is directed at land within a province, this framework gives rise to tripartite negotiations, with the federal government, the provincial government and Aboriginal peoples at the table. Thus, there is no single representative of the Canadian state, any more than in constitutional negotiations. Each level of government is a separate negotiating party at the tripartite table. Federal policy requires that Aboriginal people negotiate as a group, so that the Aboriginal party can consist of all or some of the bands making up a single nation or a coalition of bands from different nations. Just as governments do not have a uniform position at the tripartite negotiating table, Aboriginal peoples don't have one either.

In addition to these three main parties, experience over the last quarter century shows that there are other interlocutors seeking to protect interests affected by the negotiations. These interlocutors fall into two categories: public or private users holding resource licences or land development permits, whom federal policy identifies as third parties; and Aboriginal peoples that have concurrent rights or interests on the land under negotiation, which federal policy refers to as overlapping claims. Even though they are not represented at the tripartite negotiating table, these groups can have significant influence on the process. Representatives of third parties put forward their position forcefully throughout the Nisga'a land claims negotiations in British Columbia, and especially from 1990 to the conclusion of the agreement in 1998.

In some cases, different parties have common interests. For example, all parties may wish to see a clarification of the nature and extent of the ancestral rights that Aboriginals may enjoy once an agreement is reached, including Aboriginal title, as well as the conditions under which these rights can be exercised. In addition, the three parties may want this clarification to take place through a negotiated process in which each party has enough manoeuvring room to put forward its interests and positions.

Even if there is no single position representing the interests of the Canadian state, the two government parties, federal and provincial, can have common interests. First, it is clearly in the interest of both levels of government to clarify crown title to Canadian territory by eliminating the possible encumbrance of an undefined Aboriginal title. Until now, ancestral rights and Aboriginal title have been potential obstacles to development programs and activities; if they are more clearly defined in an agreement, this situation could be corrected. Second, negotiation can contribute to reducing the probability of Aboriginal legal action. As things stand, court cases cost governments time and money even when they win, while a court case that governments lose can stop development or resource extraction on the land in question. Finally, it is in the interest of both levels of government to define as precisely as possible the conditions under which the rights provided for in an agreement can be exercised.

Not only can the two levels of government have common interests, but either the federal or the provincial government can share some interests with Aboriginal people. It should not be forgotten that Ottawa adopted its land claims policy in 1973 without consulting the provinces, even though provincial interests were directly affected. Under the Canadian constitution, public lands belong to the provinces in which they are located. However, according to federal land claims policy, only Ottawa can judge whether a claim — which, in the course of events, can result in the allocation of new lands to Aboriginal people — is well founded. This is the main reason why Ottawa insists that the provinces, which need to consent to such an allocation of lands, must be at the table. Thus, negotiation of the ancestral rights of Aboriginal people takes place in a context where there is no preexisting consensus between the two government parties representing the Canadian state.

Hence Aboriginal peoples face two government parties that can have opposing positions on some subjects.

The experience of negotiations with the Attikamek and Montagnais Indians over twenty-two years has shown that the Quebec government can have interests in common with Indians. The situation has been accentuated by the strained relations between successive Quebec governments and Ottawa, which have had repercussions for the negotiations. Thus, if the Quebec government plans to carry out a large-scale project while a tripartite negotiation is going on, its interests can coincide with those of the Aboriginal party, affecting the general dynamic of the negotiation process.

The position Quebec has adopted on the extinguishment of rights is another example of common interests. For a long time, the Quebec government has stated that it does not share Ottawa's insistence that agreements have to be conditional on rights being extinguished. Ottawa has long regarded Quebec's stance as an attempt to attract Aboriginal support for its positions.

The federal government or a provincial government can also have interests in common with one or more communities that are part of the Aboriginal party to the negotiation. If a government anticipates carrying out some activity in an area inhabited by only one community, then that government's interest may coincide with that of the community in question, which could have a decisive influence on the way the negotiations proceed and whether an agreement is reached. Thus, negotiation of the James Bay and Northern Quebec Agreement led to the splintering of the Indians of Quebec Association, which had obtained an injunction on behalf of the Crees in the early 1970s to prevent the James Bay hydroelectric project from going ahead. Because the Quebec government insisted that it wanted to negotiate only the demands of the Crees, these two parties became allies and Quebec's other Indian nations were shut out of the negotiations.

The negotiations with the Attikameks and Montagnais provided more examples of this phenomenon in the 1980s. A joint council representing the two Indian nations fell apart when Hydro-Quebec reached an agreement with the Attikameks on a hydroelectric project. Subsequently, Hydro-Quebec reached an agreement with the Montagnais band at Mastuiash (Pointe-Bleue). This agreement confirmed the existence of strong centrifugal forces that made it impossible for all the Montagnais bands to get together at the same negotiating table after the collapse of the joint council. There is currently dissension between two Montagnais communities on the North Shore — which in theory are party to the same land negotiation — over another development project announced by Hydro-Quebec. Thus, the interests of the various Aboriginal communities do not always converge.

In another example of converging interests, both the federal government and the Aboriginal party — for different reasons — can prefer to have an agreement grant more land to Aboriginal people rather than provide financial compensation. Ottawa would have to pay the largest share of a financial settlement, while putting more emphasis on land would increase the provincial contribution and reduce the federal share. Such a situation could develop in Quebec, where there are Aboriginal claims to largely undeveloped areas such as the lower North Shore of the St. Lawrence, home to Innu-Montagnais communities. In other circumstances, Quebec could favour a settlement with the reverse emphasis. Thus, the Attikameks inhabit an area in northwestern Quebec where there is considerable development and resource exploitation. Here, the emphasis is on greater financial compensation since little land is available.

For the Quebec government, grants of new lands are a function of the amount of compensation and the scope of governmental powers that are agreed to — two very important elements that are at the heart of this kind of negotiation. The terms of land claims agreements generally include provisions specifying the extent of the land on which Aboriginals can exercise their rights. These rights are of different types: ownership rights on some parcels, rights of use on others, rights to take certain resources, rights to receive royalties on resource extraction. In addition, compensation is typically provided for the cession of ancestral rights and damages suffered by Aboriginal peoples as a result of development on the land they traditionally occupied. Because of the size of the lands involved and the rights that can be exercised there, concessions on these lands are a strategic element in negotiations, even more important than determining compensation. Since any such agreement involves provincial jurisdiction over land and requires provincial ratification, this question represents a constraint on Ottawa in applying its policy.

While common interests emerge in the course of land claims negotiations, each party clearly has its own interests to put forward as well. In some cases, the questions involved could be matters of indifference to the other parties. However, it must be expected that the interests of each party will sometimes conflict more or less directly with those of the other parties.

The federal government, given its constitutional responsibility for Aboriginal people, has particular interests in at least two areas. First, Ottawa needs to seek to limit the future extent of its fiduciary obligation towards Aboriginal people. The federal government's discretionary authority means that Aboriginal people are at the mercy of its decisions. Hence, Ottawa is responsible before the courts for the exercise of its authority, so that it needs to try to limit its general responsibility towards Aboriginal people by reducing the exercise of its discretionary power. A land claims agreement provides an opportunity for Ottawa to transfer government powers to Aboriginal people. As a result of such a transfer, its fiduciary obligation towards Aboriginal people can come to an end or be reduced in specific areas.

Second, it is in the federal government's interest to have the provinces assume some of its constitutional obligations, especially in areas involving land and partial payment of compensation. Ottawa has exclusive responsibility for Indians and Inuit, but the policy it adopted in 1973 had the effect of attributing part of the responsibility for settling land claims to the provinces. Because land rights are a determining factor in these negotiations, there is no doubt that the provinces assume a large share of the costs of land claims agreements.

A provincial government involved in tripartite land claims negotiations also has particular interests. It should be remembered that not all provinces are called on to participate in these negotiations. Treaties signed between the mid-nineteenth and mid-twentieth centuries extinguished Aboriginal title, on which the negotiations are based, in Ontario, Manitoba, Saskatchewan, Alberta and the Northwest Territories. Nor do all the provinces involved in the process necessarily have similar interests. A province's position in Confederation, its economic situation and its relations with Ottawa can all affect its interests in land claims negotiations. Thus, from several points of view, each province has its own interests in relation to the two other parties. Experience shows that British Columbia and Quebec, for example, do not necessarily have common positions on land claims policy.

The Quebec government sees land claims negotiations as an opportunity to broaden its jurisdiction with regard to Aboriginal people. The negotiations have allowed Quebec to subject Indians to its powers, as it has continually sought to do since 1867. Quebec sees this broadening of authority as a way of limiting federal jurisdiction in the province. The James Bay and Northern Quebec Agreement, which established an integrated structure of provincial administrative bodies, is a good illustration of this perspective.

In addition, by participating in land claims negotiations, the Quebec government seeks to prevent Ottawa and Aboriginal people from reaching a bipartite agreement on self-government in its absence, as happened in Manitoba in 1994. The Manitoba agreement specified three areas for priority projects, one of which involved education. This confirmed that Ottawa regards Indian education as an area that falls under its exclusive jurisdiction over Indians. The Quebec government expressly challenges this position, arguing that education in general, which is under provincial jurisdiction, should include the education of Indians.

In this perspective, it is important to the Quebec government to short-circuit possible negotiations between Ottawa and Aboriginal people on powers it considers its own. For Quebec, assuming costs in the context of tripartite land claims negotiations through which it can clearly establish its authority over Aboriginal government institutions may be the preferable option. In this way, it can avoid being excluded from a bipartite initiative that would establish Aboriginal government institutions over which it would have no authority.

A provincial government that agrees to participate in a land claims negotiation can also use the negotiation to make Ottawa assume political responsibility for recognizing Aboriginal rights. The federal government is in a better position than the provinces in this regard. Not being as close to the public as provincial governments, Ottawa's management of public affairs is not as subject to public reaction. Hence it doesn't have to bear the weight of its land claims policy directly. Ottawa also benefits from the fact that diverging interests in the various regions of Canada make it difficult to mobilize public opinion against a federal policy on a Canada-wide basis. Aboriginal claims are very sensitive issues for the public, so provincial governments can argue — as has occurred in Quebec and British Columbia — that this is a federal process in which they have no choice but to be involved. This argument is not necessarily convincing to a province's voters, as the situation in B.C. showed in 1998, but provincial governments can at least justify their position by maintaining that they are not the ones primarily responsible for confirming special rights for Aboriginal people.

A land claims negotiation can also serve to limit the expectations of other Aboriginal groups whose claims are pending or coming up. Since the federal policy was adopted in 1973, it has been observed that an agreement with one group typically serves as a model in subsequent negotiations. Ottawa tends to use the agreement as a frame of reference that it seeks to adapt to the specific conditions of the next negotiation. This framework becomes a constraint because it involves an effort to apply a single formula to all situations across the country. Meanwhile, for Aboriginals an existing agreement becomes a new threshold that needs to be crossed. Thus, for a long time governments regarded the 1975 James Bay and Northern Quebec Agreement as a model to apply, while Aboriginals saw it as a model for them to surpass in other claims.

The final agreement reached in 1998 with the Nisga'a Indians in

British Columbia is now producing the same phenomenon, as there are hundreds of similar claims in the province. Ironically, the model of the James Bay agreement was imposed on the B.C. government, and now the Quebec government runs the risk of having the model of the Nisga'a agreement imposed on it. It is thus very much in the interest of a provincial government facing a number of land claims to try to limit the terms of the resulting agreements. Otherwise, what from its point of view are concessions can escalate with each negotiation. Provincial governments are very sensitive to public criticism regarding any kind of recognition of Aboriginal rights. They don't want to see public hostility towards Aboriginal people become exacerbated as a result of these negotiations, as could happen if they recognize rights that most people see as privileges.

There is much to learn from the negotiations that have taken place in Quebec and British Columbia. Quebecers have become frustrated because of their government's discretion regarding the content and terms of negotiations it has carried out with Aboriginals. Land claims negotiations are not the only ones that have caused problems in Quebec. The Quebec government has been equally discreet about negotiations on sectoral agreements with particular nations. When an agreement is made public, the government often raises expectations by presenting it as a document that will resolve longstanding problems. Hence, people become even more frustrated the next time, when new problems arise or old ones involving the same nation resurface.

The B.C. government adopted a very different strategy, inviting third parties affected by the negotiations — companies involved in commercial exploitation of fish, wildlife, forests and mines, hunting and fishing associations, and others — to express their positions. The views of these parties came through loud and clear, and they were opposed to the claims of the Nisga'a. Since a provincial government is more exposed to the grumbling of the population than Ottawa is, it needs to take measures to avoid paying too high a price for the "concessions" it grants in the context of the land claims process.

In light of their current situation, and given that they carry little weight in their power relationships with governments, Aboriginal peoples may be the party with the most to gain in land claims negotiations. The negotiations represent an opportunity for them to obtain massive investments to correct their pitiful socioeconomic situation. They can use an agreement as leverage towards their future development, and so it is very much in their interest to obtain the broadest possible recognition of their rights. From their point of view, these rights should be defined in sufficiently vague terms so that they can eventually benefit from the "generous, liberal interpretation" that the courts have applied for a number of years. The Supreme Court has interpreted Aboriginal rights in this way since 1982, resolving ambiguities and doubts in favour of Aboriginal people. There is no way of knowing for how much longer the court will adopt this principle, but conceivably it will do so as long as the political situation continues to stagnate. It will probably maintain its current attitude until the rights recognized in 1982 have been implemented. Aboriginal marginalization means that this cannot happen in the short run.

Thus, the vaguer and less circumscribed the terms of an agreement are, the more likely the courts, or at least the court of last resort, will be to interpret them in a way that is favourable to Aboriginals. This does not mean, however, that any litigation involving a modern land claims agreement will be decided in favour of Aboriginal people.

Aboriginal people need to try to reach "open" agreements — that is, to avoid having their rights framed by a definitive agreement, which so far is the kind of agreement the Canadian government has signed. Under such agreements, which include the James Bay and Northern Quebec Agreement and the Northeastern Quebec Agreement that followed it, signatories give up any possibility of subsequent recourse based on the same motives. Other Indian nations roundly criticized the Quebec Crees for signing the James Bay agreement under these conditions in 1975, and the Nisga'a in British Columbia have come under similar criticism since 1998. Another significant difficulty raised by a definitive agreement is that it places enormous pressure on Aboriginal representatives to define the future of their communities once and for all, with no possibility of adjustment.

Aboriginal resistance has become stronger since 1982 because Aboriginals see recognition of their rights as incompatible with signing a definitive agreement that involves extinguishment of their Aboriginal rights. They no longer want to cede their rights, as federal policy continues to require them to do, or have those rights extinguished. Their position is that it should be possible to reevalute new agreements as their situation and the general Canadian political context evolve. They want to make sure that they will be able to benefit from any possible constitutional amendment that recognizes new Aboriginal rights.

For example, in the series of constitutional conferences that took place in the 1980s, there was no consensus on explicit recognition in the constitution of an inherent right of Aboriginal people to self-government. In this context, final land claims agreements provide for Aboriginal government mechanisms established under the authority of the federal or provincial government. These institutions are not independent, and Aboriginals accept this because they are not in a position to insist on anything else in the current political and legal situation. On the other hand, they would like to avoid being limited indefinitely to this kind of political institution and seek to preserve the possibility of replacing these institutions with independent ones if an inherent right is recognized in the constitution.

Land claims negotiations also make it possible for Aboriginal people to avoid the vagaries of lawsuits that can limit the theoretical recognition of their rights that they achieved in the 1982 constitution. The events of 1982 completely changed the perspective in which Aboriginal people view legal action. Aboriginal rights, including Aboriginal title, have been recognized, at least in theory. If Aboriginal peoples can demonstrate that their Aboriginal rights had not been extinguished as of 1982, they should be able to exercise these rights. Recourse to the courts makes it possible to specify the nature and extent of these rights, but it can also restrict their extent by defining them. This is what has happened in a large number of decisions rendered by the Supreme Court since 1982. By giving effect to Aboriginal rights, the courts both make it possible to exercise these rights and limit their exercise by circumscribing them. The *Delgamuukw* judgement is a good illustration of the fact that a court decision sends the parties back to their own devices — sooner or later they need to meet, negotiate modalities and make compromises. In other words, they need to come back to a negotiating table.

In the new context that has prevailed since 1982, constitutional negotiation is very attractive to Aboriginal people, because they no longer have to prove that their rights are recognized. Recourse to the courts does not have the same importance in dealing with these questions as it did before 1982. Aboriginal people have more room to manoeuvre in negotiation than in a legal proceeding in terms of specifying the principles that they would like to see recognized and the subjects that should be included in an agreement. They also have more control over the negotiating process itself, while in a legal proceeding they take a back seat to lawyers and judges and discussion is limited to legal questions.

Developments on the international scene over the last two decades have led to documents that recognize collective rights for indigenous peoples in terms that go beyond what states have been willing to recognize in their domestic law. It should not be surprising that Aboriginal people are inclined to refer directly to these international documents. For example, on the question of the right to political institutions and self-government, international documents envision institutions that are much more autonomous than the ones that governments in Canada are prepared to concede in land claims agreements.

Another factor also affects the course of land claims negotiations. There is a tendency to think of the Aboriginal party as homogeneous and undifferentiated, in land claims negotiations as elsewhere. Federal policy forces Aboriginal people to form groups to have access to these negotiations. There is no guarantee that these groups will be stable, and their representatives don't necessarily have the authority to negotiate in the name of the people they speak for, let alone to conclude an agreement. The effect of the insistence on forming groups is to mask the fact that the interests of the Aboriginal party are not homogeneous. Each community belonging to the group has its own interests, which could be opposed to the interests of the group or of another community.

Governments that have participated in these negotiations since 1973 have learned that this is a constant problem. It is necessary to resist the temptation to take for granted that communities that belong to the same Aboriginal nation and are grouped in a tribal council, for example, have more common interests than divergent ones. The problem is just as acute when the Aboriginal party represents different nations.

Each community has particular interests to put forward in land claims negotiations. Political and legal authority is located in the base community — the Indian band or Inuit village. Hence, the probability of a final agreement will be lessened if each community does not see some benefit for itself in both the form of participation and the content of the discussions. The feeling of belonging to a local community often seems stronger than the feeling of belonging to a nation. For a long time, this widespread phenomenon was neglected in land claims negotiations. Eventually Ottawa, taking account of the complete failure that it experienced in a number of cases, had to modify its requirements. The examples of the Dene in the Northwest Territories and the Innu-Montagnais in Quebec are typical. In negotiating the claims of both these nations, Ottawa ended up modifying their form of representation and participation. This was partly because local communities wanted to impose their respective points of view and partly because they refused to have common "national" institutions imposed on them.

Besides the interests at play, another very important element in government-Aboriginal negotiations, and especially land claims negotiations, is the quest of all parties for certainty in an agreement. A major source of friction is the difficulty of reconciling the recognition of new constitutional rights for Aboriginals with governments' wish to reach agreements that will prevent Aboriginals from having any further recourse after they are signed. The concept of certainty in land claims negotiations is not easy to pinpoint because of the numerous and divergent interests involved. It is a major challenge to come up with an explicit formulation of the concept, which may not have the same meaning and implications for all the parties. But it is precisely because all the parties are seeking certainty that it is so important to identify the interests at play. At least the amount of time and energy wasted in trying to find satisfactory formulations may be reduced if the interests and objectives of each participant in the negotiations are established at the outset.

Determining interests and objectives should make it possible to undertake negotiations in a new spirit, which would be at the heart of the new perspective that needs to reign in relations with Aboriginal peoples. There are, of course, reasons intrinsic to the Canadian situation that make it essential to work towards this end. In addition, the growing repercussions of developments in other countries and on the international scene make the need to find new solutions to Aboriginal questions in Canada even more acute.

The influence of international concerns

Aboriginal marginalization and the realization that the current system is a failure are clear enough evidence of the need for profound changes in habits of mind, attitudes and means. The actions I have suggested until now, aimed at setting such changes in motion, are ones that flow from internal factors within Canadian society. The final factor that needs to be considered is an external factor, but one that is likely to have increasing influence on the internal situation in Canada.

Globalization and the way questions related to indigenous peoples have evolved on the international scene are making it necessary to change our strategy within Canada. International public opinion and international institutions have increasing influence within states — this is a new phenomenon that will probably continue to grow. The time when governments could regard questions relating to the protection of fundamental rights as questions of internal governance alone has passed. The position of minorities, whether indigenous or not, has become a matter of international concern, expressed through international institutions, public and private humanitarian organizations and the media. Any significant disparity is likely to attract the attention of international public opinion, a global star of the moment or an international humanitarian organization. No country can escape this sort of attention. This new reality has a particularly strong impact on Canadians because there have been occasions in the last twenty years when the traditional image of Canada — and of Quebec more than any other Canadian province — has been tarnished on the international scene. Canada has long enjoyed a favourable image as a rich country. Some may see it as a little boring, but it is a country where people live in peace and there is no better country in the world.

International consciousness evolved over the second half of the twentieth century. Western countries initially recognized decolonization only as a phenomenon taking place in their former colonies — that is, affecting only people living outside the colonizing countries themselves. Increasingly, however, demands have also been heard for the recognition of political and social rights for minority peoples living within those countries. Meanwhile, national groups of indigenous people have begun to claim the status of minority peoples with the right to self-determination. They aim to win recognition of their right to govern themselves with their own institutions and according to their own rules, and in some cases even to secede from the country in which they live. Indigenous people have made increasingly frequent and prolonged representations on all the international platforms available to them. Media interest in their concerns has increased as well. The result is a new state of affairs that countries such as Canada need to deal with.

Work undertaken in the 1980s at the United Nations bears witness to the increased international interest in questions relating to indigenous peoples. In 1982, the UN Subcommission on Prevention of Discrimination and Protection of Minorities established a Working Group on Indigenous Populations. Its mandate was to study the extent of indigenous people's rights and formulate recommendations for providing better protection of those rights. After more than ten years of research and consultations with governments and indigenous groups, the working group developed a Draft United Nations Declaration on the Rights of Indigenous Peoples[1] and recommended that it be adopted.

As its name indicates, the mandate of the working group was to deal with "indigenous populations," which was the term used up to that point in instruments of international law. They were not recognized as peoples because they were regarded as communities whose members should integrate through a process of individual assimilation into the wider society of the country in which they lived. The evolution in the conception of indigenous rights that took place as the working group pursued its mandate is striking. This evolution was reflected in the wording of its suggested draft declaration, where the term *indigenous peoples* replaced *indigenous populations*. The working group wanted to declare its distance from the conception that had prevailed until then in various international forums.

The preamble to the draft declaration is explicit on this matter. In its recommended text, the working group declares not only that the discrimination indigenous people face in many countries should be eliminated but also that attempts to assimilate them should be ended and measures should be taken to ensure their collective survival in the states where they live. It sees the diversity of peoples as a contribution to the richness of the common heritage of humanity. Its suggested preamble also condemns doctrines and policies in which some peoples are superior to others. Moreover, the preamble specifies that treaties and other agreements between states and indigenous people are a legitimate subject of international concern and responsibility. The working group also recommends recognizing indigenous peoples' right to determine freely their relations with the state in which they live, in a spirit of coexistence, mutual interest and full respect. The whole draft declaration affirms the principle that indigenous people have the collective right to live freely in peace and security as distinct peoples within a state. The conception it proposes is radically different from the one that had hitherto prevailed.

The working group also took an interest in work that had been done during the 1980s by another international body, the International

Labour Organization (ILO). The revision of an ILO convention concerning the rights of indigenous and tribal populations in the workplace, originally adopted in 1957, was the occasion for extensive intergovernmental discussion on the status of indigenous people in international law. The final text of the new convention (Convention no. 169)[2], adopted in 1989, contains a preamble that addresses similar considerations to the ones expressed by the UN working group in its draft declaration. This preamble states that "developments in the situation of indigenous and tribal peoples" since the mid-twentieth century "have made it appropriate to adopt new international standards on the subject with a view to removing the assimilationist orientation of the earlier standards." It is through deliberate choice of words that the 1989 document is entitled the "Indigenous and Tribal *Peoples* Convention," rather than referring to *populations,* as its predecessor did. Thus, the ILO went through the same terminological shift as the UN working group did, in conjunction with its stated aim of "recognizing the aspirations of these peoples to exercise control over their own institutions [and] ways of life" and "to maintain and develop their identities ... within the framework of the States in which they live."

The preamble also notes "that in many parts of the world these peoples are unable to enjoy their fundamental human rights to the same degree as the rest of the population of the States within which they live, and that their laws, values, customs and perspectives have often been eroded." Therefore, the text of the convention envisions concrete measures being taken to protect the economic and social rights of indigenous people with respect for their customs, traditions and institutions. In addition, assistance to indigenous people to eliminate socioeconomic gaps between them and the rest of the population needs to be provided "in a manner compatible with their aspirations and ways of life."

Both the UN working group's Draft Declaration on the Rights of Indigenous Peoples and the ILO's Convention no. 169 on the rights of indigenous and tribal peoples present a new perspective aimed at recognizing, protecting and respecting the integrity of indigenous collectivities. Canada has not ratified Convention no. 169, because there are major gaps between Canadian practice and the provisions of the revised ILO convention, and ratification would require Canada to radically change its legislation and practices to bring them into conformity with the convention.[3] Meanwhile, the Draft Declaration on the Rights of Indigenous Peoples is still under discussion within UN structures.

These texts do not recognize the right of indigenous peoples to secede from the states to which they are subject. However, they do propose a new status for them, as distinct peoples with special prerogatives that guarantee their survival and collective development. All the work that has been done in international bodies is a clear reflection of the growing international concern about the position that states have reserved for indigenous peoples. These questions can no longer be regarded as the responsibility of states alone.

Even if these documents do not apply to Canada, they still constitute an obligatory reference point for most Aboriginal peoples in Canada. A number of Aboriginal Canadian groups have been putting forward their point of view very actively in various international bodies for two decades. In this sense, the way international discussions develop has a direct influence on what happens in Canada — at least on the positions adopted by Aboriginal representatives.

This influence can be seen in the parallels that have been drawn between the recognition of the existence of Aboriginal peoples in the Canadian constitution in 1982 and the way attitudes on these questions evolved internationally in the same decade. This is an indication of the expectations that have been created in Canada. In other words, Aboriginals in Canada believe that their status as peoples, which has now been recognized internally, should lead to the adoption of measures similar to those envisioned in the two international documents I have described. They don't easily accept the idea of swinging back and forth in a political vacuum, in which theoretical recognition of their rights in 1982 has not been followed by concrete measures.

The new international standards have set the bar very high for Canada, even if they can't be applied automatically within the country.

Aboriginal people point out that while Canada hasn't approved all of these new standards, it did participate in developing them, and therefore are demanding that Canada be consistent and amend its laws. For example, the ILO convention envisions an obligation to take account of Aboriginal customary laws in applying Canadian laws. Canadian legislation carries no such obligation. The government's obligations under Canadian law thus diverge from its obligations under international law. This is one of the gaps that could explain why Canada has not ratified this convention. There is also some confusion and ambiguity in the implication of the term *Aboriginal people* in Canada, the rough equivalent of the internationally used term *indigenous people.*

International discussions and documents have also influenced the development of relations between Quebec and the Aboriginal nations in the province since the National Assembly recognized the existence of those nations in 1985. The assembly passed a resolution calling on the government to conclude agreements with the Aboriginal nations of Quebec, which would specify the conditions under which they could exercise their "right to self-government" and allow them to develop "as distinct nations having their own identity and exercising their rights within Quebec." A number of agreements have been signed with various Aboriginal nations in the wake of the National Assembly resolution.

The resolution has brought about changes in the relationship between the Quebec government and Aboriginal people living in Quebec. The most notable change is undoubtedly the language used in the agreements reached from time to time over the years with various Aboriginal nations. The most recent agreements show this change clearly. Both the form and the content of these agreements suggest a more formal relationship between the parties, and terms are now being used that are close to those in the texts under discussion in international organizations. For example, the status of Aboriginal people as distinct nations and their right to their own institutions in certain areas are now being recognized.

When the government and Aboriginal people put their relations on a basis of "mutual respect for their national identities and each other's history and territorial occupation," it is clear that their intention is to situate these relations in a larger context using the terminology of international documents. The tendency towards a more formal relationship can also be seen in the way some of the agreements concluded with Aboriginal people have been presented publicly. Quebec's minister responsible for Aboriginal affairs arranged considerable media exposure for the agreement reached with the Mohawks in 1998, presenting it as a confirmation of the new spirit with which the Quebec government had infused its relationship with Aboriginal people.

Because attitudes in Quebec, in Canada as a whole and on the international scene have been changing and vocabulary has changed along with them, it is important to use concepts that are as precise as possible. Otherwise, the current confusion in the use of various terms relating to Aboriginal rights will only be compounded. This applies not only to legislation but also to all the texts of understandings, treaties and agreements signed by the federal or provincial governments with Aboriginal people. The vocabulary used should not leave room for the belief either that similar terms refer to different kinds of rights or that different terms refer to the same kind of rights. Clarity and precision in the terms used in legislation and agreements are essential. For example, before 1982, the term *Indian title* was generally used, while since that date the term *Aboriginal title* has arisen in the courts. There are differences in English and French usage as well: what are called *Aboriginal rights* in English have, since 1982, been referred to in French as *droits ancestraux*. Coherence in the use of these terms will make it possible to avoid giving the impression that different legal concepts are being referred to.

In the same way, it is crucial to define who holds these rights. There is currently much confusion and uncertainty about what the term *Aboriginal peoples* used in the 1982 constitution really means, as there is about the term *distinct nations* used in the Quebec National Assembly resolution. These terms do not necessarily correspond to concepts that are similar but defined differently in international law.

For example, the ILO's Convention no. 169 refers to *indigenous and tribal peoples*, but its definition of this expression does not capture the same categories as the Canadian term *Aboriginal peoples*. The same is true for the UN's Draft Declaration on the Rights of Indigenous Peoples.

The situation of Aboriginal peoples can no longer be seen as solely an internal question within Canada. It is now under the scrutiny of international bodies and organizations whose work inevitably has an effect here, if only in raising new hopes among Aboriginal people. It should not be expected that Aboriginal people will stop their international activity — quite the contrary. They have learned how effective some public international campaigns can be. It is no accident that the Grand Chief of the Assembly of First Nations, representing Canada's Indian chiefs, intervened publicly in the softwood lumber trade dispute between Canada and the United States in the fall of 2000, during the Canadian election campaign. Many people have noted that Aboriginal issues have been missing from recent election campaigns.

In the same spirit, by organizing an Indigenous Peoples' Summit of the Americas in Ottawa, before the meeting of heads of government at the Summit of the Americas in Quebec City in April 2001, indigenous peoples demonstrated increased coordination of their activities and a determination to make themselves heard internationally. Canada's Aboriginal people will not hesitate to take problems that are not dealt with at home to the international stage. The gulf between Aboriginal people and other Canadians is increasingly visible outside Canada's borders. This visibility has become a factor that cannot be neglected — one more consideration that challenges our society as it reflects on its future.

[1] Reproduced in Alexander Ewen, ed., *Voice of Indigenous Peoples: Native People Address the United Nations.*

[2] Available online at http://ilolex.ilo.ch:1567/scripts/convde.pl?C169

[3] I discuss this question in my book *Tribus, peuples et nations.*

BIBLIOGRAPHY

Canada. *Response of the Government of Canada to the Report of the Standing Committee on Foreign Affairs and International Trade: "Canada and the Circumpolar World: Meeting the Challenges of Cooperation into the Twenty-first Century."* Ottawa, 1998.

Canada. *Saskatchewan Treaty Land Entitlement Framework Agreement among Her Majesty the Queen in Right of Canada and Throne Entitlement Bands and Her Majesty the Queen in Right of Saskatchewan,* September 22, 1992.

Canada. Department of Indian and Northern Affairs. *Agreement with Respect to Kanesatake Governance of the Interim Land Base,* June 21, 2000.

Canada. Department of Indian and Northern Affairs. *Common Approach (Mamuitun),* January 19, 2000.

Canada. Department of Indian and Northern Affairs. *Comparison of Social Conditions, 1991 and 1996: Registered Indians, Registered Indians Living On Reserve and the Total Population of Canada.* Ottawa: Author, 2000.

Canada. Department of Indian and Northern Affairs. *Comprehensive Claims Policy and Status of Claims.* Ottawa, March 2002.

Canada. Department of Indian and Northern Affairs. *Dogrib Agreement-in-Principle,* August 9, 1999.

Canada. Department of Indian and Northern Affairs. *Gathering Strength—Canada's Aboriginal Action Plan.* Ottawa: Public Works and Government Services Canada, 1997.

Canada. Department of Indian and Northern Affairs. *In All Fairness: A Native Claims Policy: Comprehensive Claims.* Ottawa: Author, 1981.

Canada. Department of Indian and Northern Affairs. *Nisga'a Final Agreement,* British Columbia, Nisga'a Nation, April 27, 1999.

Canada. Department of Indian and Northern Affairs. *Outstanding Business: A Native Claims Policy: Specific Claims.* Ottawa: Author, 1982.

Canada. Department of Indian and Northern Affairs. *Sechelt Agreement-in-Principle.* Ottawa, 1999.

Canada. Department of Indian and Northern Affairs. *Statement of the Government of Canada on Indian Policy, 1969.* Presented to the First Session of the Twenty-eighth Parliament by the Honourable Jean Chrétien, Minister of Indian Affairs and Northern Development. Ottawa, 1969.

Canada. Department of Indian and Northern Affairs. Information Quality and Research Directorate. *Highlights of Aboriginal Conditions 1991, 1986: Demographic, Social and Economic Characteristics.* Ottawa: Author, 1995.

Canada. Department of Indian and Northern Affairs. Research and Analysis Directorate. *Implications of First Nations Demography.* Final Report. Prepared by Four Directions Consulting Group. Ottawa, 1997.

Canada. Department of Justice. Canadian Human Rights Act Review Panel. *Promoting Equality: A New Vision.* Ottawa: Department of Justice, 2000.

Canada. Parliament. House of Commons. *Indian Self-Government in*

Canada: Report of the Special Committee. First Session of the Thirty-second Parliament, 1980–81–82–83. Ottawa, 1983.

Canada. Parliament. House of Commons. Standing Committee on Foreign Affairs and International Trade. *Canada and the Circumpolar World: Meeting the Challenges of Cooperation into the Twenty-first Century.* Ottawa: Public Works and Government Services Canada, 1997.

Canada. Royal Commission on Aboriginal Peoples. *Choosing Life: Special Report on Suicide among Aboriginal Peoples.* Ottawa: Supply and Services Canada, 1995.

Canada. Royal Commission on Aboriginal Peoples. *Final Report.* Vol. 1: *Looking Forward, Looking Back.* Ottawa: Supply and Services Canada, 1996.

Canada. Royal Commission on Aboriginal Peoples. *Final Report.* Vol. 2: *Restructuring the Relationship,* Part One. Ottawa: Supply and Services Canada, 1996.

Canada. Royal Commission on Aboriginal Peoples. *Final Report.* Vol. 2: *Restructuring the Relationship,* Part Two. Ottawa: Supply and Services Canada, 1996.

Canada. Royal Commission on Aboriginal Peoples. *Final Report.* Vol. 3: *Gathering Strength.* Ottawa: Supply and Services Canada, 1996.

Canada. Royal Commission on Aboriginal Peoples. *Final Report.* Vol. 4: *Perspectives and Realities.* Ottawa: Supply and Services Canada, 1996.

Canada. Royal Commission on Aboriginal Peoples. *Final Report.* Vol. 5: *Renewal: A Twenty-Year Commitment.* Ottawa: Supply and Services Canada, 1996.

Canada. Royal Commission on Aboriginal Peoples. *The High Arctic Relocation: A Report on the 1953–55 Relocation.* Ottawa: Supply and Services Canada, 1995.

Canada. Royal Commission on Aboriginal Peoples. *Partners in Confederation: Aboriginal Peoples, Self-Government, and the Constitution.* Ottawa, 1993.

Canada. Royal Commission on Aboriginal Peoples. *The Right of Aboriginal Self-Government and the Constitution: A Commentary.* Ottawa, 1992.

Canada. Royal Commission on Electoral Reform and Party Financing. *Aboriginal Peoples and Electoral Reform in Canada.* Edited by Robert A. Milen. Toronto: Dundurn Press/Royal Commission on Electoral Reform and Party Financing/Supply and Services Canada, 1991.

Cumming, P.A., and Mickenberg, N.H., eds. *Native Rights in Canada.* 2nd ed. Toronto: Indian-Eskimo Association/General Publishing, 1972.

Dupuis, Renée. *La question indienne au Canada.* 1991. Rev. ed. Montreal: Boréal, 1998.

Dupuis, Renée. *Le statut juridique des peuples autochtones au Canada.* Toronto: Carswell, 1999.

Dupuis, Renée. *Tribus, peuples et nations.* Montreal: Boréal, 1997.

Enjeux arctiques pour la politique étrangère canadienne. Rapport du forum 1998 de Québec sur les relations internationales du Canada. Quebec City: Laval University, Groupe d'études inuit et circumpolaires (GÉTIC), 1998.

International Labour Organization. Convention no. 169, "Indigenous and Tribal Peoples Convention, 1989." Available online: http://ilolex.ilo.ch:1567/scripts/convde.pl?C169

McRae, D.M. *Report on the Complaints of the Innu of Labrador to the Canadian Human Rights Commission.* Ottawa: Canadian Human Rights Commission, 1993.

Political Accord between the Nunavik Party, the Government of Québec and the Federal Government for the Examination of a Form of Government in Nunavik through the Establishment of a Nunavik Commission. Montreal, 1990.

Quebec. Secrétariat aux Affaires autochtones. *Les fondements de la politique du gouvernement du Québec en matière autochtone.* Quebec City, 1988.

Quebec. Secrétariat aux Affaires autochtones. *Framework Agreement between Quebec and the Mohawks of Kahnawake Preceded by a Statement of Understanding and Mutual Respect.* Quebec City, 1998.

Quebec. Secrétariat aux Affaires autochtones. *Partnership, Development, Achievement — Aboriginal Affairs Québec Gouvernement Guidelines.* Quebec City, 1998.

Sioui, Georges E. *For an Amerindian Autohistory: An Essay on the Foundations of a Social Ethic.* Translated by Sheila Fischman. Montreal: McGill-Queen's University Press, 1992.

Soberman, D.A. *Report to the Canadian Human Rights Commission on the Complaints of the Inuit People Relocated from Inukjuak and Pond Inlet to Grise Fiord and Resolute Bay in 1953 and 1955.* Ottawa: Canadian Human Rights Commission, 1991.

United Nations. "Draft Declaration on the Rights of Indigenous Peoples." In Alexander Ewen, ed., *Voice of Indigenous Peoples: Native People Address the United Nations*. Santa Fe, NM: Clear Light Publishers, 1994.

United Nations. Committee on Economic, Social and Cultural Rights. *Concluding Observations on Reports Submitted by Canada to the Committee on Economic, Social and Cultural Rights*, December 4, 1998. Economic and Social Council Official Records, supplement no. 2, 1999.

University of Lapland. *University of the Arctic: An Integrated Plan for the Implementation of Bachelor of Circumpolar Studies, Arctic Learning Environment, and the Circumpolar Mobility Program*. Rovaniemi, Finland: University of Lapland, Arctic Center, University of the Arctic Circumpolar Coordination Office, 2000.

University of Lapland. *A University of the Arctic: Turning Concept into Reality: A Report Submitted at the Meeting of Senior Arctic Officials under the Arctic Council in Ottawa, October 7–9, 1997*. Rovaniemi, Finland: University of Lapland, International Relations, 1997.